V. G. Belinskii, Portrait by K.A. Gorbunov, oil, 1871.
(A. Radishchev Art Museum, Saratov)

Russian Biography Series, #12

VISSARION BELINSKII

By

FRANCIS B. RANDALL

Sarah Lawrence College

Oriental Research Partners
Newtonville, 1987

Russian Biography Series, 12

ISBN 0-89250-215-0

For a description of our Biography Series, write to Dr. P.H. Clendenning,
Editor. ORP, Box 158, Newtonville, Mass. 02160.

In memory of

Phillip Charles Flayderman

a Russian soul

who called this book into existence

and for

Ilja Wachs

whom the great Russians of the Nineteenth Century

would have welcomed among them

CHRONOLOGY

(All dates are given in the Old Style, the Julian Calendar of the Russian Empire, unless otherwise noted. For the New Style, the Gregorian Calendar of the West, add twelve days.)

1811   May 30, Vissarion Grigor'evich Belinskii born in Sveaborg, Finland.

1825   Belinskii leaves his childhood home in Chembar, near the Volga, and enters the academy at Penza.

1829   Belinskii, expelled from the academy, goes to Moscow and secures admission to the University of Moscow.

1832   September, Belinskii expelled from the University of Moscow.

1833   Belinskii joins the Circle of Stankevich, and works for the Moscow Telescope as a translator, then as a writer.

1834   September–November, Belinskii publishes Literary Reveries in the Moscow Telescope and secures wide recognition.

1836   The Moscow Telescope is closed by the police for publishing Piotr Chaadaev's First Philosophical Letter. August–November, Belinskii stays at Bakunin's estate at Priamukhino.

1837   Belinskii spends summer at spa of Piatigorsk in the Caucasus to treat his tuberculosis.

1837   Belinskii writes for the Moscow Observer.

1838   Belinskii, under the influence of his study of Hegel, passes through a phase of political conservatism and mental turmoil.

1839   Belinskii moves to St. Petersburg to write for Notes of the Fatherland.

1840   Belinskii resumes and intensifies his oppositionist political position.

1843   Belinskii discovers Turgenev through his poem, Parasha. His tuberculosis worsens. November, Belinskii marries Mar'ia Orlova. Belinskii publishes eleven articles on Pushkin in Notes of the Fatherland.

1845   Belinskii's daughter Olga born.

1846   Belinskii travels to Odessa for his health. Belinskii
        discovers Dostoevskii through his novel, Poor Folk.
        Belinskii moves from Notes of the Fatherland to the refounded
        Contemporary.

1847   Belinskii publishes A View of Russian Literature in 1846 in
        the Contemporary. Belinskii's son Vladimir is born and
        dies at two months.
        May-September, Belinskii makes his only trip abroad, to the
        spa of Salzbrunn in Prussian Silesia, to Dresden, through the
        Germanies and Belgium for summer in Paris and home.
        July 3-5 New Style, Belinskii writes his Letter to Gogol
        at Salzbrunn.

1848   Belinskii publishes his last major work, A View of Russian
        Literature in 1847 in the Contemporary.
        May 26, Belinskii dies of tuberculosis in St. Petersburg,
        and is buried in the Volkhov Cemetery.

CONTENTS

ACKNOWLEDGMENTS

I am above all grateful to my Amherst classmate, the late poet and Russianist, Phillip Charles Flayderman, who initiated the project for this book, who helped formulate its substance and approach, who in the manner of Belinskii "called this book into existence" and who died tragically before seeing it completed.

I owe much for general and particular encouragement to a great many people. Chief among them have been my father and mother: E. Dwight Salmon of Amherst College who first taught me about Belinskii; the late Geroid Tanquary Robinson, the late Jesse Clarkson, Ernest Simmons and George Kline, all then of Columbia University, who gave me detailed insight and a lasting interest in Belinskii in their courses; Charles Moser who persuaded me to write the chapter on *Belinskii's Critical Position* in its present form and length, and Richard Kuhns of Columbia and Robert Zimmerman of Sarah Lawrence College who read a draft of it and made helpful suggestions; Lydia Kesich and William Park, both of Sarah Lawrence, who read a draft of the chapter on *The Letter to Gogol* and tempered its excesses.

CHRONOLOGY

(All dates are given in the Old Style, the Julian Calendar of the Russian Empire, unless otherwise noted. For the New Style, the Gregorian Calendar of the West, add twelve days).

1811	May 30, Vissarion Grigor'evich Belinskii born in Sveaborg, Finland.
1825	Belinskii leaves his childhood home in Chembar, near the Volga, and enters the academy at Penza.
1829	Belinskii, expelled from the academy, goes to Moscow and secures admission to the University of Moscow.
1832	September, Belinskii expelled from the University of Moscow.
1833	Belinskii joins the circle of Stankevich, and works for the *Moscow Telescope* as a translator, then as a writer.
1834	September–November, Belinskii publishes *Literary Reveries* in the *Moscow Telescope* and secures wide recognition.
1836	The *Moscow Telescope* is closed by the police for publishing Pëtr Chaadaev's *First Philosophical Letter*. August–November, Belinskii stays at Bakunin's estate at Priamukhino.
1837	Belinskii spends summer at spa of Piatigorsk in the Caucasus to treat his tuberculosis.
1837–1838	Belinskii writes for the *Moscow Observer*.
1838–1840	Belinskii, under the influence of his study of Hegel, passes through a phase of political conservatism and mental turmoil.
1839	Belinskii moves to St. Petersburg to write for *Notes of the Fatherland*.
1840–1841	Belinskii resumes and intensifies his oppositionist political position.
1843	Belinskii discovers Turgenev through his poem, *Parasha*. His tuberculosis worsens. November, Belinskii marries Mar'ia Orlova.

| 1843– | Belinskii publishes eleven articles on Pushkin in *Notes of* |
| 1844 | *the Fatherland.* |

| 1845 | Belinskii's daughter Olga born. |

| 1846 | Belinskii travels to Odessa for his health. Belinskii discovers Dostoevskii through his novel, *Poor Folk.* Belinskii moves from *Notes of the Fatherland* to the refounded *Contemporary.* |

| 1847 | Belinskii publishes *A View of Russian Literature in 1846* in the Contemporary. Belinskii's son Vladimir born and dies at two months. May–September, Belinskii makes his only trip abroad, to the spa of Salzbrunn in Prussian Silesia, to Dresden, through the Germanies and Belgium for the summer in Paris, and home. July 3–5 New Style, Belinskii writes his *Letter to Gogol* at Salzbrunn. |

| 1848 | Belinskii publishes his last major work, *A View of Russian Literature in 1847* in the *Contemporary.* May 26, Belinskii dies of Tuberculosis in St. Petersburg, and is buried in the Volkhov Cemetery. |

CHAPTER I

CONSIDERATIONS

RUSSIA may be the most extraordinary country in the world. The clichés that have rattled around Europe for hundreds of years are all true. Russia is in fact the land of extremes, often opposite extremes at the same time. Foremost are Russia's geographical extremes – its gigantic size and Northern location, its social extremes – the few or the one who controlled everything and the hundreds of millions as dispossessed and powerless as any in the world, its cultural extremes – its massive, persistent, native, "Eastern" traditions and its élites who have created many of the supreme monuments of Western civilization, its political extremes – the greatest tyrannical machine up to its day hurled down by the greatest revolutionary movement in history which then transformed itself into an even more tremendous tyrannical machine which was simultaneously the greatest engine of revolution throughout the world, and the extremes with which foreigners approach Russia – with sublime hope or deepest fear and in either case with the strongest, most highly colored emotions.

These extremes are all so commonplace that we distrust the very statement of them. When an author refers to "the dark, romantic pageant of Russian History", the sophisticated reader fears another onslaught of purple prose, and wishes instead for sober, dispassionate, scholarly analysis.

But dispassion is iteslf an interpretive approach, not necessarily more appropriate than others. A dispassionate approach to Russian subject matter is itself an extreme interpretation, an imposition of one complex of Western values on a dramatically different culture. We study different ages and countries for different reasons. Roman painting is fascinating, but we should be cheated by a history of Rome that emphasized painting and ignored empire. The exploitation of peasants in Renaissance Florence is a moving story, but should not displace accounts of Florence's unique and marvellous arts. No one should limit a discussion of Russia to the traditional generalizations phrased in purple periods. But if a study of Russia or any major aspect of it does not illustrate and explain, precisely and in detail, the meaning of the universal convictions about the horror and the glory of Russia and its fatefulness and romance, if the language of the study does not reflect the tone and color of its subject matter, then its intended sophistication is elaborate

1

naiveté, and its would-be detachment is colossal insensitivity to the basic nature of Russian experience.

We shall be concerned with Russia in the reign of Tsar Nicholas I. This prince, at the age of twenty nine, in December, 1825, unexpectedly ascended the throne of an empire that stretched from the neighborhood of Berlin to the neighborhood of San Francisco. He ruled it for thirty years before the anxious and fascinated eyes of Europeans in their most self-consciously Romantic period.

Half the fascination of Romantic Europe with Russia was with the country itself and its culture: its immensity, its frozenness, its strange and apparently wild Orthodox Christianity, its mysterious Slavicness, its hordes of peasant serfs whose horrible oppression was broken only by their horrible rebellions, and its nobles, an unpredictable mixture of a century of Westernization and a millenium of native Russian excess. The European view of Russia was well expressed by the French historian, Jules Michelet, in his Romantically antithetical "description" of Russian noblemen weeping in an ecstasy of humane generosity at the dreams of the French socialists over dinner, and lurching out after dinner to beat their serfs to death in a drunken fury.

The other half of Europe's anxious fascination with Russia was with its Tsar himself, a fact easy to forget when the threatening tyrant has been dead for over a century. When all of Europe was wrestling with apparently insoluble problems of unstably mixed and open-endedly changing governments, Nicholas I seemed to embody one extreme ideal type of government: absolute monarchy and absolute, glacial immobility. His rule was known to be consistent with his person. Nicholas was not wild but icy: tall, blond, blue-eyed, every inch a king, military in his bearing, manners, obsessions and policies.

Russians remember Nicholas chiefly as the reactionary tyrant of his own Empire. He came to the throne in December, 1825, in blood, cannonading down an abortive liberal, constitutional rebellion by his own army officers, the "Decembrists". Alarmed by this, he devoted the three decades of his rule to perfecting the already formidable system of repression he had inherited. His became Russia's classic age of military watchfulness, police activity, spying, informing and censorship. Educated dissenters were scrutinized, censored, restricted, arrested, provoked to flee abroad, exiled to Siberia and/or killed with unprecedented thoroughness. The rebellious serfs were kept down by Cossack frightfulness. The persecution of Poles, Ukrainians, Jews, Muslims and the other minorities of the Empire earned Russia, from then on, the name of "Prison House of Peoples".

Europeans at the time had different reasons for fear. They assumed that Russia was so primitive that it naturally submitted to brutal tyranny, with only a few unfortunate Westernized noblemen objecting and being cut down. But Russia, which had defeated Napoleon and conquered Paris, was thought to be the dominant military power of Europe. Its diplomatic influence, backed by its overpowering military threat, buttressed all the reactionary princes of Northern and Central Europe and menaced the flickers of liberalism

2

even in Western and Southern Europe and in Latin America. Only in the Balkans did Nicholas's Christian sentiments allow him to support Serbian and Greek rebels against Turkish Muslim authority. If threats failed, an avalanche of Russian soldiers could smother the liberal and nationalist rebellions in Poland, then a supposedly independent state that shared only a monarch with Russia, in 1831, and in Hungary in 1849. The Cossacks might reach Paris again. No one was safe, not even Queen Victoria.

These fears evaporated at the end of Nicholas's reign during the Crimean War (1853-56) when comparatively small British, French and even Sardinian forces were able, after an admittedly tough fight, to conquer a Russian province. Respect for Nicholas's character and policies also evaporated during the reign of his son and successor, Alexander II, when the Tsar himself reversed many of his father's repressive policies for a time, curbed the police, loosened the censorship, brought juries and other institutions of self-government to Russia and emancipated the serfs. During the same reign, the nationalist and many of the liberal forces, which Nicholas had tried so manfully to restrain, triumphed in Scandinavia and Central Europe, to say nothing of the areas more remote from Russia, without any real Russian effort to prevent them. Nicholas receded into the past as the very type of the terrible but futile reactionary ruler, doomed because he tried to turn back the tide of history, which condemned him.

In this age of partially resurgent conservatism, a case has again been made for Nicholas I. His strict and disciplined reign looks much better, not only against the background of the wholesale slaughters of earlier Russian tyrants, but when put into the background by the immeasurably more horrible tyrannies and slaughters of the Communist dictators. He was the only major ruler of his time who seriously tried to make the dictates of his Christian faith a serious basis of his policies. He was conscientious and hard-working – until the physical decline at the end; the parallel to Philip II of Spain constantly asserts itself. His outlook was not the outlook of any living conservative, but his fears, that the unchecked secular, scientific and liberal tendencies of the Nineteenth Century would inevitably lead to cumulative atheism, moral decay, social and political disruption, and pan-destructive chaos and war, are no longer limited only to conservatives. And Nicholas gave his all and did more to prevent the terrible future than anyone on our horizon.

This conservative rehabilitation of Nicholas has in turn provoked a liberal counterblast. As was never the case during his lifetime or during the Nineteenth Century liberal reaction to it, Nicholas is now accused of having ruined the future by his efforts to prevent it. The argument goes that Nicholas prevented slow, "natural", liberal reform for thirty years when it might have come about in Russia with benign results as in England, ensuring that the later revolutionaries, embittered by Nicholas's repression, and working in a Russia hopelessly out of synchronization with Europe, would inevitably be driven to too rapid overturns and massive violence. These are rather iffy questions. After forty years of following the reputation of Nicholas I, I still believe that he was a limited mind and person who, very much like Philip II of Spain, tried movingly hard to do good but thereby did great evil. This book is written from that point of view, but readers should know that there is another.

A basic flaw in so many pictures of Nicholas's Russia is the concept of thirty years of an immobile, glacial Russia. The very metaphor is incorrect; glaciers move. Russia was moving, probably more rapidly than ever in its history, but this was and is obscured by the incredibly more rapid movements of Great Britain and some other Northwest European countries and of the United States. The population of the Russian Empire increased from about 36 million when Nicholas was born in 1796 to more than twice that figure, about 75 million, when he died in 1855. The gross national product increased more than proportionately. Russia became the leading exporter of food grains in the world, mostly from the Black Sea port of Odessa, which, founded as an ideal planned city in 1806, was younger than Nicholas. The gold rushes in Southwest Siberia in the 1820s were a vital factor in the growing credit confidence that made the industrial revolution possible in Western Europe. It was in Nicholas's reign that the industrial revolution came even to Russia: steamships and railroads, cotton textile machinery and the first largescale production of steel. The construction of buildings and facilities went on unprecedentedly all over the Empire. Famines and plagues swept over the land, but so did the first modern efforts at famine relief and public medicine. The rule of law and the sway of education were extended and "took" as never before, producing an entire new class of relatively humble but literate people who would inherit the future. In spite of Russia's backwardness, the standard of living went irregularly up, and in spite of Nicholas's conservatism, the proportion of serfs fell from perhaps nine tenths to less than two thirds of the population.

The failures, the defects, the holes in all this progress during Nicholas's reign were recorded brilliantly at the time by Gogol, and more tendentiously by a host of statisticians, social scientists and revolutionaries since. *Dead Souls* was imperishably true of Nicholas's Russia, but so was all the rapid change of the age.

All this makes the central paradoxes of the reign much less puzzling: Nicholas's rule was shockingly repressive, and yet it produced, first of all, the Golden Age of Russian Culture, which continued, in the hands of men formed under Nicholas, to a grand climax in the reign of his son - and secondly, the beginnings of the world's most important revolutionary movement, which, likewise in the hands of men and women formed under Nicholas, had its first grand flowering in the next reign.

Nicholas, obviously, was what some of our journalists like to call an "authoritarian" dictator rather than a "totalitarian" one. Neither his desires nor the technical capacities of the time permitted the so nearly total control of all information, thought, effort and activity which our modern Leviathan states have achieved. In spite of Tsarist Russia's then awesome network of controls, most family life, much economic activity and a great deal of intellectual and cultural creation went on independently of the regime's decree, censorship and even knowledge. There were many outer areas and inner interstices in which Russians could crouch and even walk to the horizon, as there would not be under Stalin or Hitler or Mao. One can't imagine Stalin allowing and even at times promoting, as Nicholas did, the careers and works of Pushkin and Gogol. One can't even dream of Stalin sparing the life of Vissarion Belinskii.

Belinskii, the subject of this book, was surely one of the most improbably romantic phenomena of all the romantic Russias. Even a thumb-nail sketch of his career and achievements, such as we find in a textbook or encyclopaedia, sounds like an uncritical literary effusion of the last century.

Vissarion Belinskii, we are repeatedly asked to believe, was born a nobody in the depths of cruelly caste-stratified Old Russia and rose to influence his country's future more than did the Tsar himself. Dying of tuberculosis before his career even began, Belinskii in fourteen short years, from 1834 to 1848, was the "literary dictator" of Russia. Not an imaginative writer himself, his critical writings for journals that were one step ahead of suppression by Nicholas's police almost single-handedly forged the future of Russian culture and politics. His head full of German Romantic ideology which we find incomprehensible and preposterous, he, according to its dictates, called into existence the interrelated Russian realist novel and the Russian revolutionary movement. They came upon the summons; he recognized them, established their place in Russia and in history, gave them his blessing and died young. - It doesn't really matter that even Marxists, who by their own theory should not be worshipping Great Men, say these things. They have the smack of gross exaggeration and intrinsic improbability about them, like the career of Joan of Arc.

Yet I am soberly prepared to offer you a book in which I shall affirm and try to provide detailed evidence for believing every one of the apparently fanciful propositions set forth above. On this astonishing subject I stand not only with the Communists but with Herzen and Turgenev. Let me try, in the rest of this chapter, to supply a more nearly credible outline of Belinskii's achievements, and of the ways in which they will be treated in the various chapters of this book.

Vissarion Belinskii, born the son of an obscure army medic in 1811, did indeed rise to become Russia's leading literary critic in the 1830s and 1840s. His success, however, was fatally clouded by his almost lifelong tuberculosis, of which he died horribly throughout the 1840s, the end coming in 1848, just in time to avoid arrest and Siberia at the hands of Nicholas's political police. This inspiring and tragic story will be told in Chapter 2, *A Tragic Life*.

Belinskii, by every account in what Isaiah Berlin calls "the maze of memoirs" of the period, was possessed of a luminous personality, of an improbable sainthood. He was learned and ignorant, sophisticated and naive, terrible and gentle, raging and loving, a great hater and a lovable invalid, a citizen of the world and passionately Russian, a perceptive genius and a befuddled ideologue, a senser and teller of the Truth no matter how terrible, how risky

and how wounding, a great leader and a dying child, the Prophet
Elijah and Little Nell. His personality was, in the opinion of those
who knew him, his noblest achievement, and made all his other great
achievements of critical judgment and moral-political influence
possible. No study of Belinskii can omit a comprehensive picture of
what he *was*, in the words of the literary geniuses who knew and loved
him. This picture will be given in Chapter 3, *As Others Saw Him*.

Belinskii, an intellectually and ethically serious person,
was engaged in a lifelong quest to find what was true and therefore
what was the good way for himself and for Russia. His long, shifting
and complicated intellectual pilgrimage through the minds of his
Russian friends and their German Romantic and later French radical
sources is a conspicuous part of the record he left behind him. It
is the best known part of Belinskii's activity to English-speaking
students of Russian affairs. Isaiah Berlin, Evgenii Lampert,
Richard Hare and other scholars have given us fine pictures of
Belinskii's place in Russian history and have emphasized his rest-
lessly changing philosophical and social thought. Herbert Bowman's
Vissarion Belinski (1954) has given a whole generation of American
Russianists its most detailed description of Belinskii's quest.
Victor Terras's more recent *Belinskij and Russian Literary Criticism*
(1974) has thoroughly examined Belinskii's Russian predecessors, his
German and French sources and his creative adaptations of them all.
Consequently this book will not emphasize Belinskii's successive
systems of thought, but they will be outlined in Chapter 4,
Belinskii's Critical Position. My chief purpose in that chapter will
be to show that German Romantic ideology, so alien and apparently
evil to the current Anglo-American intellectual world, was in
aspects one of the noblest creations of the human mind, and was never
more nobly and effectively adapted and used that by Belinskii in a
very different country.

In every textbook Belinskii is identified as the leading publi-
cist of the "Westerner" school in its battles with the Slavophiles
in the Russia of the 1830s and 1840s. This was dramatically true,
but Belinskii's really great public achievements, in my opinion,
were these two interrelated ones:

1. From 1834 on Belinskii shook up a complacent, provincial
and disjointed literary public, and persuaded much of it to demand
with him an authentic, national, Russian literature. This literature was to be driven, as he himself was driven, by a moral passion
for absolute truth about public and private matters. It was to deal
"civicly" and fearlessly with the dreadful realities of Tsarist
Russia, and at the same time lay bare the workings of the inmost mind
and heart, being in both "the free conscience of the Russian people".

No one person literally "calls into existence" a great literature. Surely the great Russian novelists would have written brilliantly without Belinskii. Pushkin's generation and even Gogol's
wrote or began writing without Belinskii's midwifery. But Russians
of genius and insight who knew Belinskii and the great writers he
inspired, Russians - notably Turgenev - who *were* the great writers
he inspired, repeatedly used the metaphor, "to call into existence",
an attribution almost of divine powers, to describe what Belinskii

did for the Russian prose story and novel. They repeatedly stated,
with a sensible qualification, that by the power of his calls,
Belinskii "did as much as any man" to summon that literature into
existence, that supreme Romantic achievement which we call Russian
Realism.

Having at least helped stir a number of great writers into
creativity, both noblemen and men from the lower orders whom he himself enabled to break into the formerly exclusive social circle of
Russian literature, he recognized them, however different from each
other and from himself, with almost unerring perceptiveness and
secured their acceptance by the reading public, which in turn greatly
stimulated their future writing. — These are the grand actions that
are possible when one has won the position of "literary dictator" of
a country. — When Pushkin was strangely disregarded by many
Russians, Belinskii reformulated the elements of his greatness and
compelled his recognition as Russia's national poet. In the course
of his fourteen years of dominance, Belinskii "discovered", hailed
and made famous Koltsov, Gogol, Lermontov, Nekrasov, Turgenev,
Goncharov and Dostoevskii. No critic in all history can equal that
record. Had he lived only seven more years we can be sure he would
have discovered Tolstoi.

2. Less consciously and clearly in the 1830s,but very self-
consciously from 1841 on, and equally important, Belinskii "did as
much as any man" to summon into existence that great Romantic way of
life which we call the Russian revolutionary movement. To know and
tell the truth in Tsarist Russia and so many other societies is to
stir discontent, dissent and presently revolution. The standards of
high, tense passionate, moral truthfulness, resistance to evil, and
questing for the good which he imposed on the writers led some of
them and many others straight to political action. Belinskii *was* a
revolutionary; he was the model revolutionary for three generations,
from Chernyshevskii and Dobroliubov in the 1860s through Kerenskii
and Lenin who made the Revolutions of 1917, not for his political
actions ; he was never able to perform any — but for his ethic, his
intensity, his resoluteness, his aspirations, the contents and style
of his writings, for his whole agonized life.

Chapters 5 through 9 of this book will deal with these supreme
public achievements of Belinskii's, but not in a way that has been
undertaken before. These achievements have been widely, almost uni-
versally recognized by Russians and by foreigners who know Russia,
surprising as it will seem to foreigners who do not know Belinskii.
The Russian revolutionaries and the later Communists simply revered
him. But the liberals and presently most of the conservatives also
deeply respected his pure, devoted and tragic life and his high
aspirations. They came to hold up Belinskii as the prime example of
an early, noble revolutionary before the rots of dogmatism, sec-
tarianism and violence set in, a predecessor with whom to shame not
only the Communists but also Chernyshevskii's Generation of the
1860s.

But most of the non-radical admirers of Belinskii, from the
Silver Age of Russian culture at the turn of the Twentieth Century
on, have judged Belinskii as a noble example of what a revolutionary

could be but rarely is, but a dreadful influence on Russian literature, responsible from the start for its tendentious, politicizing
faults - and as a miserable writer himself. Prince D.S. Mirskii, in
his *History of Russian Literature,* which was for the generation
between the two World Wars the classic work on its subject in
English, expressed this view vigorously:

"Belinsky's historical importance can scarcely be
exaggerated ... He was the first of a dynasty of journalists who
exercised an unlimited influence on Russian progressive opinion. He
was the true father of the intelligentsia, the embodiment of what
remained its spirit for more than two generations - of social idealism, of the passion for improving the world, of disrespect for all
tradition, and of highly strung, disinterested enthusiasm ...
Perhaps never was a critic so genuinely in sympathy with the true
trend of his times. And, what is more, he discerned almost unerr-
ingly what was genuine and what meretricious among his contemporaries.
His judgments on writers who began their work between 1830 and 1848
may be accepted almost without qualification. This is high praise
for a critic, and one that few deserve ...

"His faults, however, are also serious. First of all comes
his style, which is responsible for the dreadful diffuseness and
untidiness ... of Russian journalese ... Certainly no writer of
anything like Belinsky's importance ever wrote such an execrable
lingo. Secondly ... it was Belinsky, more than anyone else, who
poisoned Russian literature by the itch for expressing ideas, which
has survived so woefully long ... Belinsky ... is largely responsible for the contempt of form and workmanship which just missed
killing Russian literature in the sixties and seventies ..." (1)

My own teachers, notably Ernest J. Simmons, Geroid Tanquary
Robinson and Jesse Clarkson, added to this indictment the judgment
that Belinskii was the man most responsible for the studied badness
of Communist writing. There are exceptions: Herbert Bowman has kind
things to say about Belinskii as a writer and George Kline, who
knows Russian poetry as well as he has mastered Russian thought, has
been vigorous in praise of Belinskii's lively writing. The
Communists, unfortunately, have made no studied defense of Belinskii
as a writer, assuming rather that his "trenchant" style on behalf of
worthy ideas of itself constitutes good writing.

I shall therefore not follow the normal pattern of treatment
of Belinskii's writings: the selection of fragments of many pieces
from his collected works to illuminate his diverse and changing
thought and critical judgments. Russians in the 1830s and 1840s did
not read Belinskii's collected works. They read his individual
pieces as they came out, complete or in successive numbers of one of
the thick journals. The power of what Belinskii originally had to
say depended in large part on how he presented it in those journal
articles, on his style of presentation, on his writing. He knew
that, and he attempted to write enticingly, convincingly and powerfully. I shall do Belinskii the courtesy of analysing him as he
wrote, of studying five of his major works from start to finish, as
he wrote them, as pieces of *writing.*

8

As will be seen, I uphold the minority position that Vissarion Belinskii was a very fine writer indeed, who could wield every literary technique from wit to indignation, from dramatic reversal to delicate or wicked suggestion, from the stacked comparison to the thundering repetition, with great effect. Nor did Belinskii just plough on heedlessly; I believe I have detected quite complex organizations in his works, full of changes of direction and tone like the new, formally irregular works of Romantic music in his day, which also struck those who could not or would not study them as formless and badly composed.

If this minority thesis is to convince, it must be by detailed analysis of Belinskii's pieces in Chapters 5 through 9. I have chosen for such analysis first of all his *Literary Reveries* of 1834, the work that made him famous, which made him almost at a blow the literary dictator of Russia, the work in which he first sounded most of his characteristic themes. I have then selected four pieces from his later years in the 1840s, when he had arrived at his final positions that would be of lasting influence. One is his set of articles on Pushkin's *Evgenii Onegin*, published in 1844, his most extended criticism of a notable work. Next come his *View of Russian Literature in 1846* (published 1847) and his *View of Russian Literature in 1847* (published 1848), his last major work. Both of these survey a good deal of Russia and the world as well as the title subjects. Finally I shall discuss his most famous and widely available piece, known simply as *The Letter to Gogol*, which was not written for legal publication but which is certainly not a typical private letter of Belinskii's either, but rather his best known radical blast and, as was obvious when he wrote it, his testament.

This selection cannot please everyone who knows Belinskii. These five works are surely worth discussion but so are at least two dozen other major reviews and articles and some more dozens of letters. An ideal book employing my method would prove intolerably long. So be it; one must choose, and recognize the riches that have to be left out. One criterion of selection is that all these five works are at least partially available in English translation, and can be read to check up on me, and for profit and delight. In the last chapter, I shall try to give some idea of Belinskii's influence and reputation since his death.

Perhaps this discussion of Vissarion Belinskii's work and achievements helps resolve the paradoxes of Nicholas I's reign: Why did the repressions he worked so hard to impose not prevent the rise of a great revolutionary movement, as conservatives hoped they would? And why did these repressions not suppress Russian culture along with so much else, as liberals feared they would? Nicholas was not alone in Russia. Many sparrows and a number of whales fell without the will of the Tsar. Nicholas, all unwitting, presided over the nursery of an astonishing number of geniuses. Obviously Belinskii alone did not cancel the will of the Tsarist state and turn Russia in a different direction. But it is not too much to say that the flourishing writers and the budding revolutionaries of that reign did eventually work that miracle. And if they did so, then Belinskii, "as much as any man", led the movement, for it was he who most centrally formulated values, called forth talents, hailed masterworks, organized public opinion and inspired the young whose time would come in the next generation. Only at a few moments in history could such an apparently powerless individual achieve so much for and against so much.

We are tempted to theorize that it could happen in that early and still fluid state of Tsarist decline, but not, say, in any of the troubled, multiply paralyzed democracies today. That theory simply records, after the fact, that Tsarist Russia somehow, not altogether explicably, brought forth a genius who did an astonishing amount to change the world, while we, somehow, have not been so fertile. At any event, no one would choose the life of Vissarion Belinskii for himself or his child, but everyone who learns of him knows that his was one of the most marvelous lives in the whole range of human possibility.

CHAPTER 2

A TRAGIC LIFE

THE family of Vissarion Grigor'evich Belinskii came from the
Middle Volga region, where many of them had been Orthodox priests.
His paternal grandfather had risen to the not very exalted rank of
deacon. His father Grigorii, however, rejected the priestly vocation
and apparently Christianity as well; he was called a "Voltairean" and
an "atheist". The father became instead what was then called a doctor, what is better termed a medic or a sawbones, an unskilled,
unprestigious medical officer of the government. He was serving with
the Baltic fleet a year before Napoleon's invasion of Russia when his
wife gave birth to their first child, Vissarion, at the naval base of
Sveaborg in Finland, on May 30, 1811, Old Style.

After the Napoleonic wars the Russian armed forces were
reduced, and Belinskii's father could only secure a wretched position
in a wretched provincial dead-end. He became the district medical
officer in Chembar, a small town – or large village – in the mixed
forest and steppe zone west of the Volga river, about half way
between Penza and Tambov. He got into trouble first for his attacks
on the Church, but chiefly for his chronic drunkenness, violence and
cruelty to his family and patients alike. In his last years (he
lived until 1835) he is said to have refused to visit the sick for
fear that they would settle earlier scores by assaulting him. All
accounts agree that Belinskii's father was a brutal, vicious failure.

His mother Mar'ia had come from a slightly more prosperous and
cultivated Chembar family, the Ivanovs, but she herself is described
as severe, erratic and silly. She had two younger sons and a daughter, none of them remarkable. She would nag her husband for not
rising in the official and social scales even to the petty level of
her own family (ex-sergeants in the naval artillery, etc.). He would
beat her up in return, smack the children too if they were within
reach, and go out to drink some more. Chembar was a fly-speck of a
small town, sunk in mud or blown by dust, gripped by backwardness,
brutality and serfdom, lost in the millions of square miles of the
Russian plain. Stalin did Belinskii the very doubtful honor, on the
centenary of his death in 1948, of renaming the town "Belinskii". It
is difficult to see how a child in such a family and in such a small
town could ever develop a civilized mind. When he did, it is easy to
understand how he could recognize the cruel truthfulness of his
greatest literary discovery, *Dead Souls*.

11

One clue is the fact that however trivial the income and
status of Belinskii's family, they were far more privileged than the
great majority of the inhabitants of Chembar and the rest of the
Russian Empire, who were peasants, mostly serfs. The Belinskiis
were legally free subjects of the Tsar. Because Belinskii's father
was the son of a clergyman, he and his family belonged to the middle
of the five legally established castes of the Empire; they were
"honorable citizens" (*pochetnye grazhdane*). This caste, which
included the richer merchants, the middle ranking bureaucrats, the
university graduates and the professionals of the Empire, was exempt,
along with the clergy and the nobility, from paying poll taxes, from
being drafted into the army, from corvée labor at public works and
from corporal punishment. The Belinskiis did not have to work with
their hands and backs. They were never hungry. They lived in a
house, not a hut, with wooden floors, not earth. They had clean
linen and servants, though not much and not many. And they were
literate in a Russia where over 90% were analphabetic.

Much credit must be given to young Vissarion's maternal relatives, the Ivanovs. They encouraged him to spend time with them.
In their house he was spared loud quarrels and beatings. He was
never physically strong or active, and was probably a natural candi-
date for the pleasures of reading, but it must have been the
Ivanovs who communicated the beginnings of that enthusiasm for reading and literature without which he could never have become the
great Belinskii. They had him read all of their small library.
They all liked Russian poetry best; Vissarion began to write verses,
we are told, at the age of nine.

Once when he was ten or eleven his father came home roaring
drunk as usual, yelled at his son and knocked him down for no reason
at all. Vissarion later identified this particular "stupid injustice" as the occasion on which his bonds of respect for the authority
of his parents snapped. After that he was "emancipated" (a word
with a sombre meaning in a land of serfs), morally on his own.
Presumably the existence of an alternate family, of a refuge at the
Ivanovs, made this physically and psychically possible.

Even in the depths of provincial Russia there was more
schooling in the reign of Nicholas I than we are likely to think.
Vissarion was tutored by a priest and then went through the tiny
school in Chembar. Learning was on a low level, wholly by rote, and
utterly unenlightened, but it did advance the child's development.
When he was twelve, the inspector of schools for the province of
Penza reported that he was a serious student. At fourteen Vissarion
was permitted to enter the *gimnaziia*, the governmental-clerical
academy, at Penza, the provincial capital eighty miles to the east.
He was now free of his parents for most of the year, and he spent
much of his vacations with the Ivanovs.

Penza was a backwater to which metropolitan revolutionaries
were sometimes exiled (e.g. Herzen's blood-brother, the poet Nikolai
Ogarëv in 1835), but to Vissarion it was a real city, where he could
enjoy urban delights such as the theatre and amateur theatricals.
He was befriended by at least one teacher at the *gimnaziia*, a man
named Ivanisev, who could lend him a wider variety of books than

was available in Chembar: translations of the novels of Walter Scott and issues of some of the thick journals that Belinskii would later use to move all Russia.

Although he clearly learned and grew a great deal during his more than three years at the *gimnaziia*, he was expelled in 1829, at the age of seventeen, for non-attendance at classes. It is more than a little puzzling why he should have cut to this degree, for his expulsion could be expected to end his meagre prospects. He was already ill, and this must also have been the first manifestation of his lifelong inability to submit to the prescribed rules of the authorities.

Vissarion must have been an optimist, and already possessed of an iron will, for he managed to get the money from his family to go to Moscow, and there, somehow, he persuaded the authorities at Moscow University that he was worthy of admission even if he had not completed the *gimnaziia*, and deserving of a small stipend as well. This was a staggering feat for a boy nobody in the reign of Nicholas I, and if he had not succeeded, he would probably have remained a nobody. In spite of all the Communist research into their hero's life, we simply don't know how he pulled it off.

As it turned out, admission to Moscow University in the fall of 1829, when Vissarion was eighteen, was his passport to the great world. He was now forever free from his nightmarish home and from the extreme limitations and horrors of life in a remote province of Russia. From then on he would live in the two Russian capitals and associate with the most intelligent and cultivated people of the Empire. But no one could have been sure of that at the time. In an age when the status, wealth and influence of one's family meant almost everything, Belinskii brought with him to Moscow almost no assets save his modest learning, his thirsty intelligence and the resolute independence of mind that he had had to develop to survive his childhood. He was of course a neurotic, as his constant agonies of mind, his permanent timidity with men and his long-lasting inability with women testify, but all things considered, he had grown up far less neurotic than we should expect.

He came to Moscow with one more terrible legacy from his boy-hood: tuberculosis. This was the great age of tuberculosis, the central disease of the Romantic world and the Romantic imagination. It was not the fault of his wretched parents that he had contracted it, nor of their relative poverty, nor of the provincial backwardness of Chembar; tuberculosis also spread in loving families and metro-politan palaces. But the disease was taken by his friends and later by the public to be the crucial scar left by the constrictions of his background. Likewise no one could blame the continued ravages of consumption, which was to kill Belinskii at the pitifully early age of thirty six, on the police tyranny of Nicholas I, but Belinskii's tubercular life was pitied by his friends, and later by most of literate Russia, *as if* it had been caused by maltreatment during an unjust prison term, *as if* it were the expression in his life of the suffocating, choking atmosphere of the Tsarist régime.

In the Romantic age it was widely thought that tuberculosis, before it killed, granted its victims unusual mental acuity and abnormal poetic and artistic sensitivity. It was as tempting for a Russian to believe this of Belinskii as for an Englishman to feel it about Keats. It is more certain that victims of tuberculosis tended to seek each other out. This was a factor in the formation of Belinskii's friendships with a number of remarkable consumptives, notably Stankevich.

When his friends thought of Belinskii, they could never forget his tuberculosis, as is clear from the memoirs to be quoted in the next chapter. The disease was a central fact of Belinskii's life, outlook and spirit. Its unpredictable ebb and flow, its transformation of life into a chronic struggle of the most elemental sort, the inhibition of physical faculties and the apparent stimulation of the mind, the consequent highly strung nerves, high tension and simultaneous sense of great potentiality and despair – all of these coincided with and reinforced the peculiar cast of mind which many thoughtful and sensitive Romantics built up for themselves even without the disease. The Romantic-tubercular sensibility was an essential part of what Belinskii passed on to the Russian realist novel and the Russian revolutionary movement.

Having gained admission to Moscow University, the young Belinskii almost threw the immense advantage away. He attended rather few lectures and took no examinations. This was not unusual under the Continental university system of the time, and tuberculosis was also part of the explanation. But Belinskii was apparently the kind of student who found it difficult to follow the regular and prescribed courses of study and to meet official deadlines, but who threw himself into the reading of subjects that interested him and into passionate intellectual discussions with student friends. The result, naturally, was a very uneven education. He really got to know Russian literature up to that point, but was bad at foreign languages and history, and at the sciences. It was this lop-sided, autodidactic knowledge that even his friends would later call his "ignorance".

At this distance it looks as if Belinskii chose the better part. Formal education at Moscow University was on the whole hidebound and pedantic, without the distinction or the life of some of the German universities of the time. Nicholas's police wanted this to be the case. A lively university might produce more young rebels like the Decembrists, whose rising had been suppressed less than four years before. From 1826 on the régime prohibited the teaching of philosophy at Moscow and cut down on other suspect subjects. It tried to appoint only reactionaries to the faculty, and set many spies on students and teachers alike. Just after Belinskii's time it would move to reduce the student body of about eleven hundred to three hundred, so as to have fewer trouble-making intellectuals to deal with.

There were a few stimulating professors – there would be more a few years later – and some of them succeeded in sneaking a fair amount of forbidden philosophy, etc. into their lectures. But by all accounts it was the students who were the real education at Moscow University. The numerous students from the German minority in Russia were thought to be dull careerists who played everything safe. But among the Russian majority the late 1820s were one of those rare, golden moments in academic history when intellect and culture suddenly became the rage. This burst of student intellectual activity was mostly half-baked and juvenile-Romantic, but many eminent men later remembered it as stirring, marvelous and important. Aleksandr Herzen, a student at Moscow University with Belinskii, who became a great writer and the mainstay of the Russian revolutionary movement, described the scene in his memoirs:

"Thirty years ago the Russia of the *future* existed exclusively among a few boys who had just left childhood, so insignificant and unnoticed that there was room for them between the soles of the autocratic jackboots and the ground – and in them was the heritage of the 14th of December – the heritage of the wisdom common to humanity and of the purely national *Rus'*. This new life sprang up like grass trying to grow on the lip of a smoldering crater.

"In the very jaws of the monster the children are created, quite unlike other children; they grow, develop and begin to live a completely different life ... They are the initial seeds, the embryos of history ...

"Little by little groups of them are formed ... then the groups repel one another. This dismemberment gives them breadth and manysidedness for development ... the circle of Stankevich, the Slavophiles and our circle.

"The main feature of all of them is a profound feeling of alienation from official Russia, from the core of their surroundings, and together with this a drive to get out of it, and in some a powerful longing to destroy it themselves"(1).

Herzen was describing the birth of the Russian *intelligentsia,* the young people and the young in heart who were privileged or lucky enough to secure an education, who had absorbed the culture of Romantic Europe, who were therefore torn between Russia and Europe, unhappy under the reactionary regime and increasingly hostile to it, the pool of intense and alienated human beings from whom the great Russian writers, composers and artists would be drawn, from whom the Russian revolutionaries would be recruited. At this early date most of the student *intelligentsia* were sons of noblemen, but they felt it unworthy and un-Russian to stand on rank in their relations with their fellow-students. But a growing number of the *intelligentsia* were, like their future leader Belinskii, *raznochintsy* (literally "men of different ranks"), sons of the lower-middle ranks of society (but rarely of serfs) who were qualifying themselves through education for upper class careers, but who knew that they might be frozen out on account of their low origins. Their ethical outrage at the caste system was reinforced by personal insecurity and resentment.

Belinskii did not, in his university years, join the soon-to-be-famous circles of Herzen or Stankevich or the Slavophiles. He was apparently part of less organized circles whose members,

15

save for himself, would not become important. But the atmosphere was much the same. He and his friends became members of the *intelligentsia,* but they were not yet self-conscious revolutionaries. They had sympathy for the hanged and exiled Decembrists, some of whose sons and younger brothers were among them. They were furious at the many unjust penalties and expulsions visited on their fellow-students for offhand remarks that sounded subversive to the police. (Herzen's whole circle was exiled for years because some of them got drunk at a party and sang a dirty song about the Tsar so loudly that the police heard it). They drifted away from traditional Orthodoxy to a warm, humane, mushy, Romantic religion, but few were yet atheists. They had great moral objections to Russia's caste society, both the privileges of nobility and the horrors of serfdom, but few were yet republicans, fewer called for a violent revolution against the Tsar, and none was yet organizing one. Their yearnings found expression chiefly in literature, the Romantic literature of the West in its Byronic phase of defiance, and its Russian counterpart whose supreme representative was Pushkin.

The chief surviving document from this period of Belinskii's life is a play, *Dmitri Kalinin,* which is Byronic in its rhetoric and its sentiments. It is not a political play, but its hero, an illegitimate son of a nobleman, does protest against the privileges of nobility and against serfdom, and pledges never to rest while a single suffering human being remains in the world. We are told that Belinskii was still naive enough to hope that the play would earn him 7,000 rubles and secure his financial independence. His more disastrous naiveté in submitting the play to the censorship - under Nicholas I! - shows how undeveloped the emerging revolutionary movement was in 1831. The play was censored *in toto,* of course, and the attention of Nicholas's political police was now drawn to this "ungrateful" state scholarship student, to this new subversive.

More than a year later, in September, 1832, he was expelled from Moscow University for not having taken any examinations and for ill-health, of which he was guilty, for lack of ability, which may have been the authorities' honest opinion- and, clearly, although it was not stated,for being the sort of person who would write such a dangerous play. With the petty sadism characteristic of Tsarist bureaucrats, Belinskii was compelled to carry with him and submit on all official occasions a humiliatingly phrased certificate of expulsion.

Belinskii regarded his expulsion as an injustice, not as an occasion for self-doubt. He seems to have been depressed nonetheless, because he was given to depression and because his prospects were now, for the second time, quite bleak. The normal thing for such an expelled student from the ranks of the *raznochintsy,* Russia's lower middle classes, to do would have been to let one of his noble fellow-students find him a post as tutor to his younger siblings in some provincial manor house. But Belinskii was grimly determined to stay on in Moscow and not disappear forever into the bottomless provinces. He didn't even write his parents about his expulsion for seven months, probably less from shame than from fear that they would demand his return to Chembar and even use the police to bring him.

16

He accepted instead even humbler jobs as tutor to flunking students at the University and at local high schools, and as translator of short pieces – the best that his friends could get him in Moscow. Translating was particularly hard, because although Belinskii was to become a powerful intellect, he was always terrible at languages. Even in his last years he was said to know French only fairly well and German badly, a severe intellectual handicap when so little had been translated into Russian. Now in 1832 he had to tutor and translate from both languages, slowly and painfully, with a dictionary.

But in the spring of 1833, Belinskii finally enjoyed two decisive strokes of fortune. He was slowly taken into Stankevich's circle, which determined his intellectual direction, and he secured regular employment on one of the thick journals, the *Moscow Telescope*, which led to his career as a writer.

At that time Moscow was a more lively intellectual and cultural center in Russia than St. Petersburg, where the official atmosphere was too stifling and the political police too omnipresent. Among adults the crucial institutions were the *salons* run by several cultivated noblewomen and noblemen, notably Pëtr Chaadaev. Among the youth, students at Moscow University and recent graduates, the equivalent was the "circle", the group of friends that met regularly and frequently to enjoy themselves by discussing the great issues of life and books, long into the night.

The circles were less elegant than the *salons*. Women were rarely present: they would enter this world in numbers only with the "Generation of the 1860s". There was less food and more smoking, less French and more Russian spoken, fewer witty epigrams and more intensity, and ultimately a greater contribution to Russia and the world. It was slowly becoming clear that the three most important circles were those forming around the Kireevskii brothers and Aleksei Khomiakov – the future Slavophiles, around Herzen and Ogarëv who devoted themselves to political and social questions, to the emancipation of the serfs and presently to French socialism, and around Stankevich.

Nikolai Stankevich (1813-1840) was born two years after Belinskii, the son of a wealthy nobleman of Voronezh province. When he came to Moscow University, he seemed to embody Russian virtue. He gathered around him and led unassumingly the circle of remarkable friends that was the essential occupation of his life. All of them agreed that he was a marvelous and magnetic person and that the world would have lain open before him if he had not had an even worse case of tuberculosis than Belinskii. As it was, the intensely Romantic and doomed young aristocrat urged his circle, gently but compellingly, to the study of literature, art and philosophy – Schelling, Fichte and Hegel whom Nicholas's police would not let them study formally at the University.

A number of the circle were granted the time and fortune to do more than Stankevich himself: the poet Aleksei Koltsov, the historian Timofei Granovskii, the critic and inspired dilettante Vasilii Botkin, Konstantin Aksakov who later became a Slavophile writer, Mikhail Katkov who later degenerated into a reactionary

17

journalist, Belinskii himself and a late recruit to the circle
(1835), Mikhail Bakunin. Stankevich went to Germany in 1837 to
study philosophy at its source, the University of Berlin. Within
two years he was broken by his tuberculosis. He retreated to
Switzerland, tended by Bakunin's sister Varvara, to die at the age of
twenty seven. He left behind him enough articles and often beautiful letters to fill a few volumes, and a conviction among many
people that this had been the finest soul the Russian nation had
brought forth.

        Stankevich's circle became Belinskii's real home, even after
Stankevich's departure. Here he wrote his letters, and spent his
happiest afternoons, evenings and nights (certainly not mornings).
When Stankevich was alive, Belinskii wrote him that he loved him
more than the whole world. When he was dead, Belinskii told others
that he had loved him more than he now loved his own wife. Such was
the communion between two consumptives, such was Russian friendship
in the Romantic age. When Belinskii had to move to St. Petersburg
in 1839, he never got over the loss of his wonderful circle of
friends in Moscow.

        At first the members of Stankevich's circle educated
Belinskii, drew him out, led and urged him on. Later he became the
mightiest and most famous figure in it, but he still depended on
Stankevich and the others to find the important foreign books for
him, to translate their arguments and selected passages for him and
to test the first expression of his ideas.

        The classic picture of Belinskii (if one may use the word for
so Romantic a figure) is drawn from the letters and memoirs of
Stankevich's circle and its partial successor in St. Petersburg,
some of which will be quoted at length in the next chapter.
Everyone described Belinskii as a great and noble soul. He never
drank - one can understand why. He was known for his chastity,
which young Romantic men did not admire in everyone, but they
admired it in him. He had no interest in material possessions and
no personal vanity. He was plebeian and sometimes coarse enough to
grate on his aristocratic friends. He had no grace of body or movement, or of language or literary style - but he had power! The
English equivalents of his sins against the Russian language would
be the use of "different than" and "like" instead of "as". Yet
even Turgenev said that Belinskii had a literary taste superior to
Pushkin's. He was a *schlemiel*, comically awkward, shy and easily
rattled, and then his train of thought would get all mixed up and he
would stumble over his words and usually end up laughing at himself.

        But Belinskii was not only a vulnerable, lovable, grown-up
child. Everyone called him indomitable, unsubdued by either the
police or tuberculosis in spite of almost constant moral and physical pain. He was daemonically possessed of an utter, intense and
passionate honesty, sincerity and integrity of character. He *could
not* utter a falsehood, not to save himself from life exile to
Siberia, not even to avoid wounding the feelings of a dear friend.
Russians were much more impressed with this honesty and forthrightness than we are apt to be, for they lived under a tyranny that
drove everybody save a few Belinskiis to lower their voices, to

pretend that ugly realities weren't there and to lie every day of their lives.

When Belinskii wrestled with an idea, he followed it to the ends of the earth, no matter what values were shattered. When he found gold, some dangerously honest new writer, he championed him no matter who made threats – and high police officials did eventually threaten Belinskii in the streets. And when he detected stupidity, falsehood and evil, the gentle Belinskii became fierce, he hated with enthusiasm, he launched into a tirade of biting denunciations, rising from his chair and pacing up and down the room, shouting like a prophet of Israel, until he had to stop to cough blood into his handkerchief. In his writings he did not have to stop. In them he loved justice and hated iniquity until he died just in time to avoid exile. His friends therefore called him "Orlando furioso" and "Raging Vissarion" with perceptive irony, for they knew both sides of his character.

All accounts of Belinskii use the words "intense", "passionate" and "highly strung" over and over again. In the Romantic age, his friends judged this not as neurosis but as the greatness of his soul straining against the bonds of fate. Readers may be repelled by what now seems to be the excessive Romanticism of the portraits of Belinskii to be quoted from the memoirs and by the heavy doses of sentimentality in them. So be it. Belinskii really did say, "For me, to think, to feel, to understand and to suffer are the same". Belinskii really was one of the central Romantic figures of Russia.

Belinskii the man in his circle of friends was the source of his writings, but his writings took on an autonomous force of their own. In the spring of 1833 he began to translate French books and articles for the *Moscow Telescope*, one of the famous "thick journals" of Nineteenth Century Russia. In these monthlies and bi-weeklies literate Russians would find the first translations and comments on new and important European literature and thought, the serialized presentation of the emerging masterpieces of Russian literature, and as much criticism of Russian culture and the Russian scene as could get past the censor – until the day they were suppressed by Nicholas's police and new thick journals were founded. Under the police state, much of Russian intellectual life had to be spread from hand to hand and by word of mouth, but the thick journals (they really *were* thicker than books) were the major published expression of it.

The *Moscow Telescope* was edited by Nikolai Nadezhdin, a successful *raznochinets* who had just been made professor of history at Moscow University. He was acquainted with Stankevich, whose representations in Belinskii's favor, plus Belinskii's evident abilities once Nadezhdin got to know him, led from initial short commissions to regular work, to promotion from translator to increasingly important assistant editor. In August, 1834, Nadezhdin left Moscow for some months, entrusting both his thick journal and his house to Belinskii, who used his authority to publish his own first major critical work serially in the supplements of September–November 1834. This was his *Literary Reveries*, a free-flowing consideration of Russian literature and the Russian condition, which will be discussed in Chapter 5. The few thousand intellectually significant Russians, who read the thick journals, recognized "a new, strong, original talent". Belinskii's reputation was made. He was now the first member of the circles to command a national audience, the first member of the just born *intelligentsia* to dare to thunder from a national platform to move the Russian nation. Belinskii had found his *métier* at the age of twenty three.

For the rest of his brilliant career, which would not last even fourteen years, he wrote with increasing authority and influence for a succession of the most important thick journals, or rather for thick journals which became the most important because he edited and wrote for them. The *Moscow Telescope* was closed by the police in 1836 for publishing Chaadaev's *Philosophical Letter*, which excoriated Russia's backwardness and darkness in both elegant and passionate tones. Belinskii went on to the *Moscow Observer* in 1837-38. In 1839 he was lured, wrenchingly, from Moscow to St. Petersburg to write for *Notes of the Fatherland* till 1846 and for the *Contemporary* from 1846 to his death in 1848. His voice became uncertain during an intellectual and emotional crisis at the very end of the 1830s, but from 1841 he boomed uninterruptedly till the end.

While all seriously literate Russians came to read him, he was particularly "the voice of the young" and "the mentor of his generation", for whom his writings became almost cult objects. He wrote that he hoped the 1830s and 1840s would be known as "the Age of Gogol" in Russian culture. They are, but it was not only to the revolutionaries and the later Communists that they have also been known as "the Age of Belinskii".

His essential life, the life of his mind and his writings, will be discussed in Chapters 4 through 9, the bulk of this book. Let me conclude here with an outline of his less important private life.

If private life means finances, Belinskii never had much and never became prosperous. On each of the thick journals he had to slave away at time-consuming journalistic hackwork as well as write his own pieces. At the *Moscow Observer* he received 130 rubles a month, when he got it. Andrei Kraevskii, the rather crass publisher of *Notes of the Fatherland*, was accused of sweating Belinskii, the life of his thick journal, even more outrageously. In his last working year, 1847, he was supposed to get 2,000 rubles. The ruble was supposed to be worth half an American dollar through most of the Nineteenth Century, but metallic and paper rubles floated ceaselessly in exchange value and in buying power, mostly down. It is impossible to convert these sums meaningfully into current dollar values. By the standards of his day and place, they allowed Belinskii only a very grubby lower middle class living. If he was between jobs or if he had to go to a spa for his tuberculosis, his wealthy friends had to chip in.

If private life is used in the narrow modern sense of sex life, the chaste Belinskii did not provide good copy. He was rightly convinced that his body and personality were unattractive to women, and he didn't think it fair for a consumptive to marry a healthy woman. No doubt all sorts of neurotic inhibitions combined with the "Victorian" morality that was spreading even in Russia and with his revolutionary's respect for women to preserve his chastity.

When he visited Bakunin's estate at Priamukhino in Tver province from August through mid-November, 1836, he lived for the first time in a gracious noble home in daily association with upper class ladies. Bakunin's sisters, sweet *and* intelligent, charmed and melted him. He seems to have fallen into an ethereal Romantic love with one of them, Aleksandra, while another, Tatiana, fell into an ethereal Romantic love with him. These relations were broken up rudely by Bakunin when he at length noticed them, not out of class prejudice, most of their mutual friends insisted, but because of Bakunin's "personal peculiarities", by which they meant his own psychopathic relations with his sisters.

Belinskii's ideals for marriage involved a complete equality of intellect, spirit and conduct, very revolutionary in his day, and hard to live up to when so few women were educated and almost none, save George Sand whom he greatly admired and publicized in Russia, were truly emancipated. During his crisis at the end of the 1830s he confessed to "vulgar debaucheries" when in a state of despair. Apparently he picked up a few prostitutes in May Square in St. Petersburg.

Belinskii's eventual marriage had more to do with tuberculosis than with sex or his ideals. In the spring of 1837 his wealthy friends Stankevich and Botkin collected money to send Belinskii for a summer at the spa of Piatigorsk in the Caucasus, where the waters were (mistakenly, of course) supposed to help consumptives. Thus at the age of twenty six he saw his first mountains, although he was hardly able to climb in them. His health did for some unknown reason improve and his impressions helped him to appreciate the Caucasian poems and novel of Lermontov, which he was about to discover. Any benefit was undone by his move to St. Petersburg in 1839. Moscow, before it became a great industrial city, was often blessed with clear, dry, sunny days, especially during the Siberian winter cold, a good climate for arresting tuberculosis. St. Petersburg, however, was usually damp and cloudy or foggy, as bad for consumptives as London.

By 1843 Belinskii knew he was dying. In November he married Mar'ia Orlova, a young lower-middle class Muscovite woman he had met the previous summer. She was in no sense his intellectual equal and neither was her sister who moved in with them in St. Petersburg. He was not Romantically in love with her, and he wrote her so before the wedding. He "confessed" to his friends in her presence that his marriage "lacked ideal motivation and was devoid of poetry". He admitted that he had probably married her because he knew he needed a nurse. He had found a splendid nurse. She served him with a doting, submissive, mindless, Russian devotion, and was by most accounts an immense help and comfort to him. She bore a daughter, Olga, in June, 1845. His friends were amused to see the famous Raging Vissarion on his hands and knees with his daughter riding on his back. She bore a son, Vladimir, in March, 1847, who died two months later, which broke his father's heart.

None of this helped his tuberculosis. In the summer of 1846 he was given the money to make a leisurely journey south to Odessa and back, which did seem to help, but not for long. In 1847 he got an advance on his salary and gifts from friends, and left in May, without his wife, for his only trip abroad, to the spa of Salzbrunn in Prussian Silesia, supposedly good for consumptives, which, of course, didn't work. It was at Salzbrunn that he wrote his famous last *Letter to Gogol*, his most widely read and influential piece among the coming generations of revolutionaries.

He was not able to appreciate Dresden, Berlin, Cologne, Brussels or Paris when he got to them, the cities of fabulous Europe which Belinskii, like all literate Russians, had longed achingly to see. He spent two months (July-September) in Paris, chiefly with the Herzens, Turgenev, Bakunin, the memoirist Pavel Annenkov and a doctor who was thought to be a quack but who did actually seem to have done some good.

Belinskii returned to St. Petersburg and soon collapsed. He had to dictate the second half of his last major work, his *View of Russian Literature in 1847*. He sensed the importance of the revolutions of February, 1848, in France and March, 1848 in the Germanies, but he could do nothing. These revolutions frightened Nicholas I into a paranoid frenzy of brutal police repression, extreme even for his reign. His political police drew their net around Belinskii, collecting "incriminating" writings and telling his neighbors that it was not safe to associate with him. But they held off arresting the obviously dying man for fear of the disgusted reaction of the public. Belinskii finally died on May 26, 1848, Old Style, just four days short of his thirty seventh birthday. General Dubelt, the head of the Third Section of His Majesty's Chancery (the secret political police), was informed of the death and is reported to have said, "Too bad, we would have sent him to a fortress and let him rot". He sent police spies to see who attended the sad little funeral and burial.

Vissarion Belinskii was buried in the Volkhov Cemetery in south-eastern St. Petersburg, which was then rather obscure and unfashionable. Thirty five years later, Turgenev asked to be buried next to Belinskii, and around this core has grown up one of the great pantheons of the Russian nation, the "Path of Literature", on or near which are buried Saltykov-Shchedrin, Garshin, Leskov, Pisarev, Dobroliubov, Mikhailovskii, Mendeleev, Pavlov and many only less famous figures, a major pilgrimage site in Leningrad to this day, a holy place of the human mind.

CHAPTER 3

AS OTHERS SAW HIM

BELINSKII *was* one of the noblest souls and most colorful personalities of Russia's greatest century, but more than that, one of his foremost achievements was his ability to inspire many great writers to describe him, memorably and delightfully. In sum, the verbal portraits of Belinskii are the greatest character study of a real Russian that has come down to us. Part of the explanation is the very fact of Belinskii's early death, which left many of his friends with twenty to forty years of active life in which to remember Belinskii in association with their own lost youth and to polish their memories of him. Part of it is their conviction that in describing Belinskii, they were describing the best of the Russian national character caught in the unique tragedy of the Russian condition. Part of it is inexplicable: fire struck fire to make a splendid light.

It is sacrilegious but necessary in a short book to omit most of this treasure house of material. It particularly hurts to have to pass over the reminiscences of Konstantin Kavelin, a friend of Belinskii's although a conservative theorist and historian, and of Dostoevskii. Pared to the bone, I can present only some passages from the three finest memoirs of Belinskii, those of Turgenev, Herzen and Annenkov.

Ivan Turgenev was "discovered" by Belinskii in 1843, when he read the manuscript of Turgenev's as yet unpublished first significant work, the long poem, *Parasha*. Belinskii championed it and encouraged its author, who, more than any other of Belinskii's discoveries, needed such encouragement to settle into his vocation about which he had a deep internal diffidence. They met and became as striking a pair of Unlike Friends as any that parade through Turgenev's later novels: the aesthetic twenty five year old nobleman and the volcanic thirty one year old plebeian. Only four and a half years later Belinskii left Turgenev in Paris to go home to Russia and die. The chapter in Turgenev's *Literary and Secular Reminiscences* entitled *Reminiscences of Belinskii* was written in 1868. It contains the most striking personal description of Belinskii that we have:

"I shall describe his appearance ... He was a man of medium height, at first glance rather unhandsome and even awkward, with a

hollow chest and bent head. One shoulder blade protruded more than
the other. Everyone, not just doctors, immediately recognized in
him all the main symptoms of consumption, all the so-called *habitus*
of that terrible disease. He coughed almost continually. He had a
small, palish-ruddy face, an assymmetrical nose as if it were
flattened, a slightly twisted mouth, little, close-set teeth; his
thick, fair hair fell in a lock over his white, beautiful but low
brow. I never saw eyes more exquisite than Belinskii's. Blue, with
golden sparks in the depths of the pupils, his eyes, most of the
time half closed, widened and glittered when he was animated; when
he was gay, they took on an enchanting expression of hearty kindness
and untroubled happiness. Belinskii's voice was weak and husky but
pleasant; he spoke with a peculiar accentuation, gutterally,
'dogmatically, excitedly and hurriedly' [a line from Nekrasov]. He
laughed from his soul, like a child. He loved to pace across the
room, tapping his snuffbox of Russian snuff with the fingers of his
small and beautiful hands. If you saw him only in the street, when
in his snug cap, little old threadbare fur coat and down-at-the-
heels galoshes he went along quickly and uncertainly hugging the
walls, and looked this way and that with the timid sternness
characteristic of nervous people - then you could get no proper idea
of what he was really like ... Among strange people in the street
Belinskii was easily embarrassed and flustered. At home he usually
wore a gray *surtout* and in general kept himself very neat. His way
of speaking, manners and gestures reminded one vividly of his background; everything in his bearing was purely Russian ..." (1).

But most of Turgenev's essay is a series of vignettes of
Belinskii's soul:

"Belinskii was a really passionate and really sincere man,
which is rare with us, capable of unselfish enthusiasm, but devoted
exclusively to the truth, irritable but not egotistical, able to
love and hate disinterestedly ... The soul of this cynic was bash-
fully chaste, tenderly soft and chivalricly honorable; his life was
almost monastic and wine never passed his lips ... It is impossible
to imagine the degree to which Belinskii was truthful with his
friends and with his own self; he felt, acted, existed only on the
basis of what he recognized as truth ..." (2).

"The outlook of Belinskii was not broad; he knew little and
there is nothing surprising about that ... The poverty surrounding
him from childhood, his bad upbringing, his unfortunate circumstances, his early illnesses and then the necessity of earning his bread
by work done rapidly - all this prevented Belinskii from getting a
solid education ... Belinskii was what I might call a *central
nature*; his whole being was close to the heartbeat of his people; he
embodied it fully, in both its good and bad sides ..." (3). "He
confused the elder Pitt (Lord Chatham) with his son, William Pitt
... so what! ... For his proper tasks he knew enough" (4).

"As with all people with souls on fire, with all enthusiasts,
in Belinskii there was a large dose of intolerance. He did not
admit, especially when aroused, a single particle of truth in the
opinions of his opponents, and he turned away from them with the
indignation with which he abandoned his own opinions when he found

them mistaken ... In general Belinskii knew how to hate - *he was a good hater* [in English in Turgenev's text] and despised with his whole soul what was worthy of contempt" (5).

"His own mistakes Belinskii admitted without reluctance; there was no trace of petty vanity in him. '*Nu*, I sure spouted blither!' he would say with a smile ... Belinskii did not have too high an opinion of himself or his abilities. His modesty was absolutely pure-hearted ..." (6).

There was no more sensitive ear than his; no one felt more vividly the harmony and beauty of our language; a poetic epithet, an exquisite turn of phrase immediately attracted his attention, and to hear his simple, slightly monotonous but burning and truthful reading of some poem by Pushkin or Lermontov's *Mtsiri* was a true joy. Prose, especially by his beloved Gogol, he read worse and his voice soon weakened" (7).

"Painting he did not understand and he was very weak on music ... The Devils' Chorus from *Robert the Devil* was the only tune Belinskii knew; In unusually lighthearted moments he would hum the diabolical refrain in his base register" (8).

"Here and there one could detect a tendency toward coarse joking and clownishness ... Belinskii himself would say he was not a master of humor, his irony was very clumsy and heavy; it soon turned into sarcasm and hit you not on the eyebrow but in the eye. And in conversation, as with pen in hand, he did not sparkle with wit, he did not have what the French call *ésprit*; he did not dazzle by the play of skillful dialectic; but in him dwelt that irresistible force which comes from honest and unbending thought, and it expressed itself originally and, ultimately, absorbingly. Completely lacking in what is usually called eloquence, and openly unwilling to 'decorate' things and throw in fine phrases - Belinskii was one of the orators of the Russian people if we understand 'oratorical ability' in the sense of strength of conviction ..." (9).

"Belinskii, undoubtedly, possessed the main qualities of a great critic ... His aesthetic sense was almost infallible; his judgment penetrated deeply and never became obscure. Belinskii was not deceived by appearances or circumstances - he submitted to no influences or set ideas; he instantly recognized the beautiful and the ugly, the true and the false, and with fearless courage he pronounced judgment, pronounced it outspokenly, without a reservation, warmly and powerfully, with all the drive and assurance of conviction. Anyone who has seen the critical blunders into which even remarkable minds have fallen (remember Pushkin, who saw in *Marfa the Mayoress* by Mr. Pogodin 'something Shakespearean'!) must feel respect for the precise judgment, correct taste and *instinct* of Belinskii, for his ability to 'read between the lines' ... At the appearance of a new talent, a new novel, poem or story — no one before Belinskii or better than he ever gave a truer appraisal, a more authentic, decisive word. Lermontov, Gogol, Goncharov - was he not the first to recognize them and explain their significance? And how many others?" (10). Turgenev was perhaps not completely modest in leaving his own name out of this list; he knew that every

Russian reader would think of him in connection with it. His exclusion of Dostoevskii is more interesting.

"Belinskii, as is well known, was not inclined to the principle of art for art's sake". Turgenev recalled the "comic fury" with which Belinskii had attacked Pushkin for two lines in the latter's *The Poet and the Mob*, in which the poet scorns the mob for valuing a pot on the stove with dinner in it more highly than poetry. "'Of course', declared Belinskii with flashing eyes as he ran from corner to corner, 'of course it is dearer. I don't just cook my dinner in it for myself alone; I cook for my family, for another poor man like me - and rather than admire a beautiful statue - even if it's an Apollo by Phidias himself - it is my right, my duty, to feed them - and myself, too, in spite of all these gentlemen and versifiers!'" (11).

"He was tormented by doubts. I often heard that phrase and used it myself more than once; but in reality it fully applied only to Belinskii. His doubts really did torment him, deprive him of sleep and food, ceaselessly bothered and gnawed him ... Once when I had just arrived, he got up from his couch, haggard and ill ... and in a voice that was hard to hear, coughing continuously, with his pulse beating a hundred times a minute, with a fevered flush on his cheeks, he began the conversation where it had ended the day before. His sincerity worked on me, his fire spread to me, I was carried away by the importance of the subject; but after talking for two or three hours, I weakened, the lightmindedness of youth asserted itself, I wanted a rest, I thought of taking a stroll, of dinner, Belinskii's wife begged her husband and me to take a little rest ... but it was not easy to deal with Belinskii. 'We haven't yet decided the question of the existence of God', he said to me at once with bitter reproach, 'and you want to eat!'" (12).

Turgenev's last memories of Belinskii in Salzbrunn and Paris were of course very sad. "The things in Paris which so strongly impress many of our fellow-countrymen revolted his pure, almost ascetic, moral feelings. Only a few months of life remained to him. He was tired and had lost interest ..." (13). Turgenev finished his reminiscences of Belinskii by quoting Mark Antony's last speech in Shakespeare's *Julius Caesar*, as several other writers would, "This was a man!" (14).

Fourteen years after Belinskii's death Turgenev dedicated *Fathers and Sons*, which he knew would be his masterpiece, "to the memory of V.G. Belinskii". Twenty one years after that, Turgenev died in France; on his orders his body was taken back to Russia and buried in the Volkhov Cemetery in St. Petersburg next to Belinskii.

*   *   *

Alexandr Herzen had met Belinskii thirteen years before Turgenev did, when they were both students at Moscow University,

26

but they did not really become acquainted until Belinskii joined
Stankevich's circle, which Herzen sometimes visited, although he was
running a rival circle of his own. Herzen was in exile much of the
time from 1834 to 1840, and when he met Belinskii again in St.
Petersburg in the latter year, he was shocked at Belinskii's temporary moral toleration of the Tsarist régime. He broke off personal
relations on good revolutionary principle, but by winter Belinskii
had wrestled himself beyond that position, and apologized to Herzen
in his open, honest way. "From that minute until Belinskii's death",
Herzen wrote in his memoirs, *My Past and Thoughts,* "we went hand in
hand" (15).

"I regard Belinskii as one of the most remarkable figures of
the period of Nicholas ... After the gloomy article of Chaadaev
appears the suffering Belinskii, bitterly skeptical and passionately
interested in every question. In a series of articles he discusses
everything, relevantly or irrelevantly, always true to his hatred of
the authorities, often rising to poetic inspiration. The book under
review served him for a good part of the material as a starting
point, but half way down the road he abandoned it and plunged into
some other question. For him the poetic line, 'That's what relatives
are' from *Onegin* is enough to summon family life before the court and
smash blood relationships to smithereens ... How faithful he is to
principle,how fearlessly consistent, how dexterously he navigates the
shoals of the censorship, how bold his attacks on the literary
aristocracy ... on the secretaries of state for literature ...
Belinskii whipped them without mercy, demolishing the self-love of
the conceited, limited writers of eclogues, lovers of culture, bene-
volence and tenderness; he made jokes of their dear, *soulful* thoughts,
their poetical reveries flowering under gray hairs, their naiveté
hidden under the ribbon of an Anna decoration. How they hated him
for it!" (16).

"The articles of Belinskii were awaited convulsively by the
youth of Moscow and St. Petersburg from the 25th of each month.
Five times the students would call at the cafés to see if *Notes of
the Fatherland* had come in yet; the heavy issue was passed from hand
to hand. - 'Is there an article by Belinskii?' - 'There is' - and it
was devoured with feverish interest, with horse laughs, with arguments - and three or four convictions, *reputations,* disappeared.

"Not without reason did Skobelev, the commandant of the
Fortress of St. Peter and St. Paul, say jokingly to Belinskii, when
they met on the Nevskii Prospect, "When will you come to us? There's
a warm cell on the shore side at my place all ready for you' (17).

Unlike the liberal Turgenev, Herzen was a revolutionary. In
his memoirs he brought out the revolutionary sides of Belinskii's
views and effect, but when describing Belinskii's character, he
clearly knew the same man Turgenev remembered.

"Belinskii was very shy and usually lost his composure in an
unfamiliar or very numerous company ... He sometimes appeared at
the literary-diplomatic *soirées* of Prince Odoevskii ... Belinskii
was completely lost between some Saxon ambassador who didn't understand a word of Russian and some official of the Third Section who

understood even words that remained unspoken ... One New Year's Eve
Belinskii would have left, but a barricade of furniture hemmed him
in, he somehow got stuck in a corner, and a small table was placed
in front of him with wine and glasses. Zhukovskii [an eminent
nobleman, poet and tutor to the Crown Prince] in his formal white
trousers with gold lace trimmings sat catty corners from him. For a
long time Belinskii endured it, but, seeing no improvement in his
lot, he began to push the table a little; the table moved at first,
but then tipped over and crashed to the floor; a bottle of Bordeaux
with all deliberate speed began to pour over Zhukovskii. He jumped
up, the red wine trickled down his pantaloons; all hell broke
loose ... Belinskii escaped and, near to death, ran home on foot.

"Dear Belinskii! How he was angry and bothered by such
incidents ...

"But in that timid man, in that puny body, dwelt a mighty,
gladiatorial nature; yes, he was a powerful fighter! He could not
preach or lecture, he had to have an argument. If there was no
opposition, if he was not annoyed, he did not speak well, but when
he felt himself goaded, when one of his cherished convictions was
challenged, when his cheeks began to quiver and his voice to rise,
then he was well worth seeing; he leaped on his opponent like a
leopard, he tore him to pieces, made him ridiculous, made him piti-
ful, and while he was at it developed his own thought with unusual
power and unusual poetry. The quarrel would often end in blood,
which flowed from the sick man's throat; livid, gasping, his eyes on
the man he was talking to, with a shaking hand he would put his
handkerchief to his mouth, profoundly humiliated, annihilated by his
physical weakness. How I loved and how I pitied him at these
moments!

"Persecuted financially by literary businessmen, persecuted
psychologically by the censorship, surrounded in St. Petersburg by
rather unsympathetic people, wasting with a disease which the Baltic
climate made murderous, Belinskii became more and more irritable ...
His strength gone, he would often come to our place to rest; lying
on the floor with our two year old child, he would play with him for
hours on end ..." (18). Russians knew tuberculosis was contagious,
but Russian friendship was stronger than the fear that the friend
might infect oneself or one's children.

It was Herzen who preserved the best version of the most
famous anecdote about Belinskii's ferocious integrity:

"Once he went to dine with some litterateur during Holy
Week; lenten dishes were served.

"'When', he asked, 'did you become so religious'?

"'We eat lenten dishes', answered the litterateur, 'solely for
the sake of the servants'.

"'*For the servants?*' burst out Belinskii and he blanched.
'For the servants?' he repeated and threw down his napkin. "Where
are your servants? I'll tell them that they are being deceived;

an open vice is better and more humane than this contempt for the weak and uneducated, this hypocrisy in support of ignorance. And you think that you're emancipated people? You're on the same level as all the tsars, priests and slaveholders! Goodbye, I don't eat lenten dishes to manipulate people, I have no *servants*!'" (19).

If this seems more boorish than highminded, one must remember the intensity of the police repression that produced the all-encompassing hypocrisy of Nicholas I's Russia as a defense mechanism. The litterateur was not fooling his servants to save their feelings but to avoid the chance that they might report his unorthodoxy to the police. One should also remember that Belinskii could have been sent to Siberia for these words alone. Herzen's next anecdote makes Belinskii seem even more grimly ferocious:

At another literary *soirée* a Russian German was annoying Herzen and Belinskii by attacking, in a vile and oily reactionary way, Chaadaev and other men who had dared criticize aspects of the Russian scene and who had therefore been victimized by the police. Belinskii was furious:

"'How sensitive we are! People are flogged - we don't mind, they are sent to Siberia - we don't mind, but here Chaadaev, you see, has ruffled people's honor - he mustn't dare speak out; speaking out is insolence, a lackey must never speak out! ...'

"'In civilized countries', said the German with bottomless self-satisfaction, 'there are prisons in which they confine madmen who insult what the whole people respect, and they do it splendidly'.

"Belinskii swelled up, he was terrifying, great at that moment. Folding his arms over his sick chest, and looking straight at the German , he answered in a hollow voice:

"'And in still more civilized countries they have a guillotine to execute those who think that's splendid'.

"Having said this, he sank into an armchair, exhausted, and was silent. At the word 'guillotine' the host turned pale, the guests were uneasy ..." (20). Again, Belinskii could have been sent to Siberia for these words alone, and so could the whole company if one of them had been a police spy and had turned them all in for not turning Belinskii in, which is why they were uneasy. Presumably Herzen approved of Belinskii's reference to the guillotine because it invoked the terrible justice of history, not because either of them was planning a Stalinist bloodbath.

"I saw him for the last time in Paris in the fall of 1847. He was very ill, afraid to speak aloud, and it was only in rare moments that his previous energy revived and his dying fire glowed hot. At such a moment he wrote his letter to Gogol.

"The news of the February Revolution found him still among the living. He died, taking its glow for the dawning day!" (21).

*   *   *

Pavel Annenkov (1812-1887) was born into the middle nobility. He was an inspired dilettante in the highest sense of the term. He sampled university life and government service, but threw up his career "to live the way I want to". What he wanted to do was to become acquainted with all the interesting people in the intellectual and cultural worlds of Russian and Europe, and for more than forty years he succeeded as well as any man. He moved in all the Moscow circles and knew most of the writers, Gogol best of all. He knew most of the revolutionaries, though a law-abiding liberal himself. The revolutionary Pëtr Lavrov later denounced Annenkov as an "aesthetic tourist" and warned other revolutionaries against him. He was a loyal Russian friend, however, and sometimes he buckled down to writing fine books, such as his biographies of the young Pushkin and of Stankevich. He is best known for his *Literary Reminiscences*, published in 1880, about what he called, coining the phrase, "the remarkable decade, 1838-1848", during which, as he described it classically, Russian literature and dissenting social thought came of age, the Age of Belinskii, who, along with Gogol, was the central figure of the book.

Annenkov first met Belinskii in the fall of 1839, when the latter had just moved to St. Petersburg. "I confess I was surprised when ... they showed me that the one named Belinskii was a gentleman short of stature, stoop-shouldered, with a sunken chest and rather large, thoughtful eyes, who very modestly, simply and in an unforced comradely way answered the greetings of the new people being introduced to him ... It was evident that beneath that exterior lived a proud, indomitable nature that might break out any minute. In general Belinskii's awkwardness, his tongue-tied and flustered talk when meeting strangers, at which he himself laughed so much, had like his whole person much in them that was expressive and engaging; behind them was the steady light of his noble, integrated and independent character ... He was quiet, preoccupied and - what particularly struck me - he was unhappy". (22).

Annenkov saw Belinskii not only with his friends, but also at home and at work. "Belinskii ... found a place on the Petersburg side of the river ... in a nice wooden house with a large but cold, damp room and a small, terrifically hot study ... Belinskii gave himself over to his thoughts and lived a very solitary, almost ascetic life, from which he came out from time to time into the circle of his new acquaintances ...

"However ... Belinskii did not then manifest any need for company ... He stood for days and nights at his desk. His rather narrow, roasting study with his desk between two windows also had a small couch and a small stand on the opposite wall five or six paces away. Belinskii almost always wrote, as was required for journal articles, on one side of a half sheet and stopped when he finished it. Then he would lie on the couch and read a book, after which, replacing the now dry sheet with another, he would take up his pen anew ... Whether he was in a hurry or not, that was how he composed his articles, tiring himself physically far more than mentally" (23).

Annenkov later recorded Belinskii's married life, declining

health and continued fire. "His daughter and then a son who didn't live very long and carried with him to the grave his father's last strength, and also the flowers in the windows were the objects of his care, efforts and most tender concern. They alone were his life, which was beginning to recede from him and leak away. Soon he had to wear a respirator when he went outside, and he joked with me, 'See how rich I've become! Maxim Petrovich in Griboedov ate off gold, but I breathe through gold: that's still grander!'" (24).

"How many times we would find him after he had finished a book, an article or a chapter, pacing through his three rooms with every sign of extraordinary agitation. He instantly started an improvisation without restraint, setting forth impressions from his reading. I found his impressions better than his articles... To judge by the number and mass of sensations, excitements and thoughts that extraordinary man lived through every day, one might call his brief life, so quickly consumed before our eyes, a reasonably long and full one" (25).

Annenkov was present when Belinskii was in the very act of discovering a great writer: "On one of my visits to Belinskii before lunch ... I saw him from the courtyard of his house, at his living room window with a big notebook in his hands and all the signs of excitement on his face. He saw me too and shouted, 'Come quickly, great news!' 'This manuscript you see here', he went on after we had greeted each other, 'I haven't torn myself away from it in two days. This novel by a talented beginner - what this gentleman looks like and how sharp his mind is I don't know yet - but the novel reveals such secrets of life and such characters in Russia as no one has dreamed of before it. Think, it's our first attempt at a social novel and done as extraordinary artists do it, that is without suspecting what's going to come out of it. The plot's simple: it deals with kind-hearted people who assume that to love the whole world is a great pleasure and a duty for each human being. They just can't understand it when the wheel of life with all its regulations rolls over them quietly and breaks their limbs and bones. That's all - but what drama, what characters'. Oh, and I forgot to tell you, the artist is called Dostoevskii, and I'm going to show you some samples of his motifs right now'. And Belinskii began, with extraordinary pathos, to read the passages that most impressed him, giving them even higher intensity by his intonation and nervous reading" (26).

And almost immediately, Belinskii set to work to write in praise of the still unpublished manuscript of Dostoevskii's *Poor Folk*.

Annenkov was in France when he heard that Belinskii had been driven to try the waters at the Salzbrunn spa. He realized that Belinskii, alone and unable to speak German, would flounder miserably. With the magnificent freedom of a nobleman and the kindness of a Russian friend, he rushed to Germany to take Belinskii in hand, as did Turgenev.

"I hardly recognized Belinskii. In a long overcoat, and a cap with a straight visor, and with a thick cane in his hand - before me stood an old man who at times ... would quickly straighten up and pull himself together ... He was, evidently, an organism

31

already half destroyed. His face had become smooth and white like porcelain ... His terrible emaciation and hollow voice completed the impression, which I tried to hide as best I could ... Belinskii seemed to have noticed my pretense" (27).

Even more awful to Annenkov was Belinskii's despair in the face of death. "I remember how once after a particularly horrible day of coughing, as he was getting ready for bed, he suddenly began to talk in a quiet, half gloomy but firm tone: 'To be sick and dying with the thought that nothing will remain after you in the world – that's the worst of all. What have I done? I wanted to finish a history of Russian national poetry and literature, but there's nothing to that now ... I know what you want to say', he went on, noticing my movement, 'but two or three articles, half taken up with ephemeral trivia already unnecessary, don't constitute a legacy ...'" (28).

Annenkov was with Belinskii in Salzbrunn when they received the letter from Gogol that stirred Belinskii into composing his famous blast, the *Letter to Gogol*. It was Annenkov who left us the full account of its composition, as will be discussed in Chapter 9. It was Annenkov who shepherded Belinskii through the Germanies and Belgium to Paris, recording pathetic details of Belinskii's trip to Europe, which had come too late.

In Paris Belinskii turned sadly away from the Place de la Concorde, realizing that he no longer had the energy to appreciate such things. Like Turgenev, Annenkov recorded that the unlimited opportunities for fashionable sex, which made Paris such a magnet for most Russian travelers, intensely disgusted the chaste Belinskii. The very size and bustle of the city oppressed him. "The impression produced in him by Paris was one of wonder and gloom ... He asked his friends, 'does civilization have to have such huge and stupefying centers of population as Paris and London ...?'" (29).

Annenkov last saw Belinskii when he put him on the train from Paris to Brussels, the first leg of his return journey to Russia. He made Herculean and successful efforts to retrieve the favorite dressing gown that Belinskii had left behind him in his nervousness, and to deliver it to him. Annenkov had bought a whole set of the new inventions, educational toys, for Belinskii to take home to his surviving child, and was wrenched to hear in a letter that they had almost been confiscated at the Belgian border. It was the last kindness that Annenkov was able to do for his beloved friend.

CHAPTER 4

BELINSKII'S CRITICAL POSITION

BELINSKII was a literary critic and his great effect beyond literature was worked through literary criticism. But his literary criticism was very unlike ours. Our critical center, the detailed and formal analysis of literary language and texts, is almost absent from Belinskii's writings, and the larger philosophical, ethical and political concerns which were inextricably intertwined with most of Belinskii's literary discussions have rarely been seen in our criticism since T.S. Eliot, or, at latest, Lionel Trilling. Any discussion of Belinskii's critical position must be at least half a discussion of the philosophical foundations of his literary convictions.

Belinskii's immense influence was not just the effect of his own personality, ideas and writing. He transmitted, reinforced and was reinforced by, mediated and modified many overwhelming cultural currents from the Romantic Europe of his century. His ideas were ideas whose time had come. For Russia, he was the voice of the best of Germany and France. Russians regarded him as the Russian climax, or as an early Russian climax of pan-European movements whose bandwagon magnetism was irresistible. We must study the sources of his ideas, for they were a significant part of the explanation of both Belinskii's immediate and lasting influence.

Everyone who writes on Belinskii tells how he was successively and overwhelmingly influenced and transformed by Schelling, Fichte, Hegel, the Left Hegelians and the French socialists. This raises a paradox, for his French was only fairly good, and he couldn't really read German philosophers in the original, at a time when few of their works had been translated into Russian, and many could not be published there on account of Nicholas's censorship, notably Hegel and the Left Hegelians. We know the solution of this paradox, Belinskii's membership in his circles. Stankevich studied Schelling and later Hegel, discussed them, preached them and made handwritten translations of crucial sections of them for himself and for Belinskii. Bakunin plunged into Fichte and then Hegel, and flooded Belinskii with them. From 1840, Herzen returned from his exile in Vladimir and immersed himself in the Left Hegelians and the French socialists; Belinskii absorbed them through him. Botkin in the 1830s and Annenkov in the 1840s were immensely helpful and obliging in supplying Belinskii with translations and explanations of what he needed. Very strictly speaking, Belinskii's sources were not the German and French thinkers but his Russian friends.

But these were highly intelligent and stimulating men, and through them Belinskii really was able to comprehend the line of giants of Romantic thought. But they were European and he was Russian. It was stirring for Herder and his successors to formulate German Romantic nationalism and set forth the nature and history of German literature, but none of them gave a thought to Russian literature, which was Belinskii's subject. Earlier and older contemporary Westernized Russians had begun the process of applying Western categories of thought to Russian phenomena - Prince Odoevskii at whose party Belinskii spilled the wine, Nadezhdin, his chief at the *Moscow Telescope* - but most of that work had yet to be done when Belinskii took up his pen.

Some of Belinskii's convictions and sentiments remained constant throughout his active career. Others evolved through a series of stages, and still others wobbled quickly back and forth. What are the sources of the thought of a man who constantly changed his mind? Of course Belinskii was a Romantic who believed in embodying many of the contrary tendencies of real life, and as a Romantic he was an evolutionist who believed that all things should change, including himself. This paradox, too, can be answered.

Belinskii liked to think of himself as a conscious heir of all that was best in Russian and European history, but in outlining his intellectual position, one may start with the French Enlightenment. He was the very type as well as leader of the "Westerners", the Westernized, "secular humanist" Russians of the 1830s and 1840s, who took their ideas and much of their behavior not from any Biblical, Christian or clerical source or model, but from the Western European tradition of the cultured gentleman, developed from the Renaissance on. Neither they nor their Western models were usually atheists - Belinskii was not definitely an atheist till 1841 - but they were not, from the mid-Eighteenth Century on, fundamentalists of any branch of Christianity.

Whatever "The Enlightenment" means, it must mean that one's picture of the world comes no longer from any church but from scientists, and one's beliefs about the good life for the individual and for society come from the tolerant, cultivated, rational, secular best behavior and writings of European gentlemen in the last few hundred years. And the Enlightened French insisted that the churches were not only false but terrible, oppressive, persecuting engines of evil, the prime enemy of all civilized human beings.

Because of Nicholas's censorship, Belinskii was never able to blast the Russian Orthodox Church in print, and even in his private correspondence, only his most famous letter, to Gogol, expressed his full anti-clerical venom. But he was, in fact, never religious, neither in childhood nor in his Hegelian period from 1838 to 1840. All his writings reveal a mind utterly secular in sentiment and tone. The source of this basic secular, anti-clerical cast of Belinskii's mind was his family and earliest teachers, and through them, very definitely, the French Enlightenment. The great French name he invoked when the censorship let him was Voltaire's, used to suggest the whole secular Enlightened movement, not just Voltaire's specific contributions to it.

The other half of the Enlightenment was "the religion of humanity", "the party of humanity", the position on what from the French Revolution on has been called the left. The persecuting churches were thought to be hand in glove allies of the unjustly privileged and oppressive nobles, serflords, monopolists, bureaucrats, censors, police, armies and the monarchical kingpins that held them all together. Belinskii's heart was always in the left camp from his teens on, though he was not a full-fledged radical democrat till 1841, and never so red a revolutionary as the Communists would like to have him. Communists play down Belinskii's great debt to the German idealists, for ideological reasons, but they are right, I think, to emphasize more than most Western scholars do Belinskii's basic rootedness in the Enlightenment.

And so we come to Germany, for Belinskii was a Romantic in the great German tradition. He did not use the word that way – he saved "Romantic" to refer to the more effusive and sentimental literature of the period 1800-1830, which he didn't much like. But historians of culture now use "Romantic" like "Gothic", as a term for a major epoch of European culture, heralded by Rousseau, emerging first in the Germanies, then in Great Britain and in all Europe, comprising most of the manysided cultural outburst of the late Eighteenth and the entire Nineteenth Centuries, in several successive phases, a later one of which we may still be living in. For decades Anglo-Americans have despised most German Romantic thought, judging it to be partly meaningless abstract drivel and partly vicious proto-Nazism. In showing what a noble soul such as Belinskii was inspired to by German Romanticism, I hope to strike a small blow to rehabilitate what was one of the great creative epochs of the human spirit.

In contrast to other writers on Belinskii, I maintain that the German Romantic who had the greatest influence on Belinskii was the first, Johann Gottfried von Herder (1744-1803). Herder, like Belinskii, had risen from low estate in an eastern province of his country. Herder, a high-intense, gloomy, irritable pastor from East Prussia, became "The Voice of the North", the prophet of the renovation of the German nation, the inspirer of Goethe and Schiller, as much as any man the formulator and caller-forth of the mighty German Romantic movement of the following 180 years. In his first important work, *Fragments on the New German Literature* (1767) and his culminating work, *Ideas of the Philosophy of the History of Mankind* (1784-91) Herder was the prime source of the German Romantic doctrines of nationality, the evolution of nations, cultural struggle, the nature of the Poet and the evolution of literature, which were the themes of the Romantic movement which obsessed Belinskii and dominated his work. Here and not in the Enlightenment were the sources of Belinskii's views of nation, literature and the function of the critic (what Victor Terras has called organicity or the organic theory), which determined most of his actual work.

It was Herder who first proclaimed in a high intellectual and resounding Romantic way that humanity is divided fundamentally into separate nations, as Belinskii would believe. A nation, for Herder, was a people characterized by a common language, history and culture, but not necessarily by a common religion or unified state; he was of course thinking of Eighteenth Century Germany. Belinskii thus had authority for excluding Orthodoxy as part of the essence of the Russian nation. Nations, thought Herder, were often in fruitful conflict with one another; Germany's antagonist was France, and Mediterranean culture generally. For Belinskii, Russia's fruitful antagonist was Europe as a whole.

It was Herder who enunciated the first of many great Romantic doctrines of evolution: human history is divided into national histories, which move ineluctibly forward in successive stages, each rooted organically in the previous stage and in all that had gone before. Everything in a nation evolves interconnectedly, stage by stage, including its very language (Herder was a great philologist) and its spirit. Central to a nation is its culture. Although Herder was mightily sensitive to music and the visual arts (He thought the German nation had been magnificently expressed in its Gothic buildings and in Dürer), he made the arts of the national language central: its intellectual and imaginative literature. These would be Belinskii's beliefs about Russia.

The truly great German literature, Herder insisted, was that of the pagan epics and the High Medieval period, whose spirit was worthily preserved in folk poetry and fairy tales. (Belinskii did *not* follow Herder here, and thought less of early Russian literature and folk tales). A great, organically integrated literature is informed by one spirit, which evolves with the nation as a whole, stage by stage. A great poet, a term Herder and the German Romantics used for any high writer, as they used "artist" in an even wider sense, is imbued with and supremely expresses the spirit of the nation in a given age. So Belinskii thought.

German literature had been in a depressed stage for almost 200 years. It might fruitfully adapt much from its antagonist France, but the 17th-18th Century Frenchification was too much and had reduced German literature to the rhetoric of a foreign French spirit not at home on German soil, prettified, frivolous and debased there. In contrast to French-Mediterranean classicism, German poets should summon up the spirit of the North, foggy, forested, still partly pagan, Ossianic, Gothic – and reclaim and rebuild their own. This Herder (rightly) thought was being done before his eyes, in a stage that promised a new, mature German literature soon, not just folk songs but a German literature that was supremely national and as high-civilized as anything French. In this process the critic (Herder himself?) had a vital role in formulating, summoning, recognizing and hailing the new stage of culture and its geniuses. As Goethe progressively revealed himself to his teacher and friend, Herder hailed him as a great genius who was making it possible for Germans to make the transition immediately to the adult, rich, widespread and triumphant stage in their literature. These were exactly the views that Belinskii would hold about the nature and development of Russian literature, about Pushkin and Gogol, the center of his critical position.

Herder's ideas were adopted by almost every German Romantic, and by Belinskii's time they were common assumptions of the whole movement. Belinskii read little of Herder and mentioned him

36

infrequently, thinking of these ideas as German in general. But it is fascinating to see how Belinskii selected from German Romanticism for his own credo, almost all the important ideas which Herder had originally contributed to it, straining many non-Herderian Romantic thoughts out. I suggest that it is very fruitful to think of Belinskii as the Russian Herder, to some degree in his personal situation, much more so in his mind, aims and achievements. This also implies that Herder was the more original and greater man.

Compared to all this, Belinskii took much less from Immanuel Kant (1724-1804), again through later German and Russian intermediaries. Kant's conviction that aesthetic experience is a distinctive kind of experience not reducible to moral or theoretical experience had its place in Belinskii's glorification of literature. Kant's conviction that a judgment of taste is possible only if we presuppose certain conditions, one of which is that it be disinterested, was extended by Belinskii to form an argument against censorship. Kant maintained that aesthetic experience has a superabundance of sensual material and a paucity of conceptual material, that the aesthetic is inexhaustible, that beauty is one piece of evidence for our supersensible nature, that creativity must be free, and free to give rules of its own making, spontaneous and unrepeatable, and that genius is the capacity to do so - and Belinskii used versions of this complex of thoughts to magnify literature, to defend its autonomy not only against censorship but any constricting ideology, and to help explain the achievements of supreme writers such as Pushkin and Gogol. Kant asserted that geniuses do more than reproduce nature; they restructure it and forge a new reality; Belinskii said these things of Pushkin and Gogol and believed that Turgenev, in falling short of them, fell short of true genius. All these propositions became the common property of most German Romantics and were assumed, from them and with them, by Belinskii, usually without any direct attribution to Kant.

It is hard to isolate anything which Belinskii took specifically from the greatest of the German Romantics, Johann Wolfgang von Goethe. He read him in such translations as he could get, loved him and admitted him to the tiny company he called geniuses, argued against him at times, and wrote a fair amount about him, but the sentiments he quoted favorably from Goethe were mostly the ones which Goethe in turn had imbibed from Herder. Goethe's original ideas within the German Romantic tradition, especially his Olympian "Classicism", were not usually followed by Belinskii.

The specific influence of Friedrich von Schiller (1759-1805) is much easier to see. Belinskii, like all Romantic Russians, loved Schiller's poems and plays, and both admired and loved to argue with his theoretical essays, though he somehow did not grant him the status of genius. The most heart-warming side of Schiller for Belinskii and for leftists everywhere was his strong, joyous drive toward freedom which would uplift individuals and all humanity. Schiller's plays that championed human freedom, *The Robbers, Don Carlos* and *William Tell*, and his *Ode to Joy*, which contained the greatest and moving line of poetry for the whole left Romantic world, "All men are brothers", had the same inspiring effect on Belinskii that they had earlier had on Beethoven. And Schiller, who was

plunged from the joyous heights of his marriage to fifteen years of
hell and death by tuberculosis, Schiller the greatest of all the
Romantic consumptives, could not fail to move Belinskii to tears.

Schiller's noble conviction that art is profoundly emancipating, civilizing and uplifting fired Belinskii's similar conviction.
Schiller saw human lives enmeshed in necessity, but we can be free
in art. The greatest art is that in which the poet freely accepts
necessity and voluntarily expresses reality. This was to be very
important for Belinskii's conception of the proper relation of art,
reality and politics. Most commentators attribute the themes of
freely obeying necessity and voluntarily portraying reality, in
Belinskii and his successors up through the Communists, to the
influence of Hegel. In fact, Belinskii and the earlier figures in
this tradition were prepared to have these convictions reinforced
and expanded by Hegel because they had already found them so inspiring in Schiller. Likewise, Schiller, before Hegel, preached art as
the union of the ideal and the real, and Belinskii followed him.
He wrote about the negative ideal in connection with comedy, and
Belinskii developed this when discussing Gogol's comedy. And
Schiller's famous and protean distinction between "naive" poetry –
early, primitive, Classical, impersonal, realistic, objective,
sculptural, including the mature Goethe – and "sentimental" poetry –
modern, sophisticated, Romantic-before-the-word, personal, self-
conscious, introspective, musical, including most of Schiller himself – found its way into Belinskii's writings.

The last of the three great and influential German Romantic
writers was E.T.A. Hoffmann (1776-1822), the author of the fantastic
tales which are not only great Gothic romances but which stand at
the head of all later European (and American) explorations of that
baleful territory in which the grotesque, the terrifying, the supernatural and the psychotic meet – not only Gogol and Dostoevskii
whose Hoffmannesque sides gave Belinskii so much trouble, but later
giants as varied as Poe, Kafka, Bulgakov and the authors of science
fiction. Belinskii knew the power of Hoffmann, but he was on principle skeptical that his was the path for literature to follow.
Belinskii sometimes mentioned the "Serapiontic principle", derived
from Hoffmann's novel, *The Serapion Brothers* – that every poetic
creation and all its parts must come authentically from the poet's
own aesthetic consciousness – but this was a rephrasing of an idea
of Herder's.

Of the influences of the German Romantic idealistic philosophers, that of Friedrich Wilhelm Schelling (1775-1854) came first.
Schelling was the chief German figure being studied by Stankevich
and his circle when Belinskii joined it in 1833, and Belinskii is
often called a Schellingian from then until 1837, after which
Schelling's influence was shared with other German philosophers, but
never disappeared. Schelling's thought was adopted by many political conservatives in Germany and the rest of Europe, and by the
Slavophiles in Russia. It was natural that when Belinskii became a
thoroughgoing leftist in the 1840s he would retreat somewhat from a
man he now regarded as tarnished.

But paradoxically, the theses of Schelling about art which

Stankevich and Belinskii adopted in the 1830s served very well in the later Belinskii's and all later Russian leftists' literary criticism, right up through the Communists. Schelling maintained that a work of art was a microcosm of its subject, and that great works of art were microcosms of great subjects, significant aspects of the life of a nation or of a whole nation, significant portions of humanity or of all mankind. It followed from this that a character or a situation in a work of art was the author's comment on the corresponding part of life. A self-sacrificing wife in a poem was a tribute to all womanhood; a corrupt official in a play or novel was an attack on all officials in the country. This was one of the principles by which Belinskii interpreted and therefore championed Gogol's *Inspector-General*. It is, of course, the critical principle which Tsars, Communists and other tyrants use to justify censorship.

Schelling insisted that great artists really represent things, absolutely and authentically grasp and present reality. This was more than a metaphor, more than high praise; it was a philosophical principle. This tremendously high conception of a writer's power lies behind a great deal of what Belinskii said about the achievement and effect of Pushkin and even more of Gogol. Schelling's theses that the artist's creations are themselves nature and can influence the rest of nature meant that a writer could be very influential by grasping his nation's condition and making its reading public realize it, thereby pushing, moving, transforming and shaping that nation anew. Schelling intended no political radicalism, but his theses have been the great faith of left artists and writers ever since, especially in Russia. It was the central tenet of Belinskii's, and what he hoped to achieve in Russia. Herzen expressed it even more memorably, "A great writer is a kind of second government of his country."

In 1836 Bakunin's discovery of and obsession with the thought of Johann Gottlieb Fichte (1762-1814) spilled over onto his close friend Belinskii. Bakunin had translated much of Fichte's crucial work, *Some Lectures of the Vocation of the Scholar* (1794) for the *Moscow Telescope*. Many of Fichte's ideas on literature and criticism were close to Schelling's and reinforced what Belinskii had already derived from Schelling. But Bakunin's great Fichtean interest, his famous doctrine of the ego, was new to Belinskii: our lifelong vocation is for each individual to cultivate and upraise himself to ever higher and more harmonious perfection. Our moral duty is to help friends and all other individuals in society to achieve that high purpose. The special duty of the scholar is to formulate and champion that ideal of the noble, whole person. Bakunin seems to have been narcissistically emphasizing the first of these theses. Belinskii took most from the second and third, conflating Fichte's ideal of the scholar with his own role as a critic. These high-minded resolves stayed with Belinskii long after he left the study of Fichte, and took on an increasingly political cast. The first glow of Belinskii's interest in Fichte coincided with the first bursting of Lermontov onto the Russian literary scene, and much of Belinskii's thinking about Pechorin and other Lermontovian characters was done in the light of Fichte's ideas of the noble ego.

At last one comes to the formidable Georg Wilhelm Friedrich Hegel (1770-1831). It can now be seen that much of what is usually

said to be the Hegelian influence on Belinskii - and on Marx, and on
the Communists - was solidly in the German Romantic tradition before
Hegel and in other German giants in his active lifetime, notably the
crucial complex of ideas about the organic interconnectedness of
things, organically developing, stage by stage evolution and fruitful conflict and struggle. Hegel was the mighty culmination of
German Romantic thought, not its originator. But once Belinskii or
any other Nineteenth Century intellectual was gripped by Hegel's vast
synthesis of German Romantic thought with all his own special ideas,
emphases and language, the entire tradition tended to be crystalized
for him in its Hegelian form. So it was with Belinskii.

The most famous instance of Hegel's influence on Belinskii,
invariably discussed even in one page summaries of Belinskii's
career, is incredible to us. We are told that Belinskii, beginning
his study of Hegel, read his most famous statement which had already
passed into epigram, "What is rational, that is real, and what is
real, that is rational", believed it, deduced that if this were true,
then the tyranny of Nicholas I, being real, must be rational and
right, and he forthwith went out and became a reactionary for two
years until he snapped out of it in 1840 by reinterpreting things as
a Left Hegelian.

Things don't happen that way. Not just this epigram
(apolitical in its context) but the whole cast of Hegel's political
thought and support for the Prussian monarchy, down to his dying
blast against the British Reform Bill, made any serious study of
Hegel a serious consideration of political conservatism. Many factors forced Belinskii to the crossroads at the end of the 1830s:
worsening health, neurosis, poverty and the bleak prospects for the
as yet unorganized political left.

For two years Belinskii did tone down his otherwise lifelong
oppositionism. Some of his pieces, notably his reviews of *The
Anniversary of Borodino* and *Sketches of the Battle of Borodino* (1839)
were not only patriotic evocations of this most ghastly battle of
the Napoleonic Wars but were outright loyal panegyrics of the
Russian monarchy. His friends were shocked and angry; their attacks
wounded him deeply. This political stance, like the phase of psychic
instability it reflected, could not last. Belinskii made existential decisions to return to the opposition, implacably and perma-
nently, in 1840-41, and he found that what he was overwhelmingly
bent to do seemed intellectually justified by choosing from the
interpreting Hegel's awesome body of thought after the manner of the
Left Hegelians he was just learning about.

Belinskii's critical position, too, had bent and in part
reversed itself under this initial shock of Hegel. In *Menzel, a
Critic of Goethe* (1840), he argued as he had not before and as he
never would again, but in line with Hegel, *against* literature that
was politically and socially relevant, up-to-date, detailed, concerned and engaged, *against* writers who plunge in to try to influence
and reform public opinion. His model in this essay was Goethe, the
middle and late Goethe who was aloof, detached, altitudinous,
Classical and Olympian. This too would pass.

Belinskii's lasting debts to Hegel were less dramatic. He

adopted Hegel's formulations about how the greatest men were "world-historical individuals", but preferred his own Peter the Great as a type example to Hegel's Napoleon. Several of Hegel's literary ideas persuaded him. Hegel believed that successive stages of society were reflected in the dominant literary genres of each stage as well as in their content. The epic flowed from early, stable, integrated societies. Eighteenth and Nineteenth Century epics were either failures because they were out of synchronization with their societies or were successful but mis-classified examples of other genres. Belinskii used this formulation in his battles with the Slavophiles, who had called *Dead Souls* the Russian epic.

Hegel judged what we call German Romantic poetry and drama (*He* did not use "Romantic" in that way) to have been products of a tumultuous time of rapid change in German history, an art coming to an end by about 1830. Belinskii, with the advantage of writing ten to twenty years later, judged that this was true of Russia as well as of Europe. Hegel thought that what was coming to its end was art as it had been, art in the service of the Spirit, art which played a central role in the community's expression of its self-consciousness He thought that what was emerging was a new type of art, which would no longer be tied to the historical drama of the Spirit's unfolding, or the unfolding of human self-consciousness, but which would be largely about itself, a free play of tones, colors, etc. Belinskii did *not* adopt this as his prognosis of the next stage of literature. Instead, he noticed that Hegel had elsewhere spoken well of recent prose stories and novels, not the fantastic tales of Hoffman but Goethe's great work on the formulation of a human mind and character, *Wilhelm Meister*. So Belinskii played a little fast and loose with Hegel, and put these two separate pieces of Hegel together with inspired insight: he proclaimed that the dawning era of Russian (and European) society was calling forth the realistic prose novel.

The last waves of foreign intellectual influence on Belinskii came at the beginning of the 1840s. Once again, through Herzen, Bakunin, Botkin and Annenkov (Stankevich was now dead) Belinskii studied the German Left Hegelians and the French socialists. The two groups were by no means identical, but Belinskii took from them what they had in common. To the Communists' relief and joy, Belinskii now, from 1841 on, became a thoroughgoing atheist, oppositionist and radical. None of this could find its way directly into print in the Russia of the 1840s, but the maze of memoirs and Belinskii's many surviving letters make this clear. Was he also a materialist? Probably, but his statements to this effect seem to have been part of his anti-clerical stance rather than sober philosophical or chemical materialism in the manner of the greatest of the Left Hegelians, Ludwig Feuerbach.

What had Belinskii's politics become? The negative side of it is clear enough: away with Nicholas I and all other tyrants, all privileged classes and all oppressors of the people and the free spirit! But what was he *for*? A completely free, democratic republic, certainly with weak central powers. There is no serious discussion in Belinskii's writings of the ways to get to the free future. Would he have accepted a constitutional monarchy along the way? His own journalism and the realistic novel were the first steps, but what would come next? Underground organization? Violence? There is little clue. Belinskii sympathized with the Poles, but left no detailed plan for their future or that of the minority nationalities in general who constituted over half the population of the Russian Empire.

He was equally unconcerned with the economic organization of society. He was interested in the French socialists of the 1840s, but was he a convert to socialism himself? His most important friend of that decade, Herzen, became Russia's first socialist, and discussed it with Belinskii in his intense Russian way. If a socialist is a man who opposes private property, this whole discussion was twisted in Nicholas's Russia where the chief form of private property was in human beings. Belinskii ragingly opposed that, but living at the very beginning of Russia's industrial revolution, he had little to say about factories, stocks and bonds. Even the Communists who are so loyally eager to claim Belinskii for their own have had to be content with calling him a "radical democrat".

None of these issues are problems in literary criticism, but he had to think about their obvious literary consequences, the degree to which literature should advance the great cause of human freedom, even at the sacrifice of other values, artistic values. Neither the German nor the French left was crudely for booming political propaganda works instead of true art, and neither was Belinskii. But the internal psychic and moral pressures to see progressive content in works that were more complicated (such as *Dead Souls*), to praise works that were strongly for freedom and weaker elsewhere (such as Herzen's *Who is to Blame?*), and to play down works that were well done but apolitical (such as Goncharov's *An Ordinary Story*) made Belinskii's later criticism strained, contradictory and fascinating.

*   *   *

I hope this review of what Belinskii took from the German Romantics makes them seem less proto-Nazi than we have often thought, and if their language was often abstract, I hope it can also be as concrete and moving to us as it was to hundreds of thousands of sensitive and ethical people in their own day. The German Romantics provided a general model of what culture, artists and critics could be for a nation, and a specific blueprint of what they could be for Germany. Most staggering to our quite different presuppositions, Herder, Goethe, Schiller and their many successors *did* it for Germany, did it *all*. Adapting that model to Russia, Pushkin and Gogol (only partly consciously) and Belinskii and the realist novelists (fully consciously) did the same things in Russia, which is almost more staggering to our presuppositions. This towering abstract edifice of impossible Quixotic idealism became sober but magnificent reality not only once but twice. Anglo-Americans still feel that such things could never have happened.

The way to make the Russian sequence of cultural events

clear is to approach Belinskii's critical position from another angle, to survey his critical estimates of the successive stages and figures of Russian literature in the rest of this chapter. Then his concepts of Russia and Russian literature in general and of all these stages and figures will be illustrated in detail in the following five chapters of analysis of his most striking works.

Belinskii departed most from the German model at the beginning. He was proud of some aspects of Old Russia but it was the modern period that was the center of his Russian nationalism. Correspondingly, he admired Russia's Twelfth Century epic, *The Tale of the Host of Igor*, the *byliny* - Russia's heroic ballads - and Russian folk and fairy tales, but they were not his central literary enthusiasm. He did not think they were a continuous enough or integrated enough tradition to constitute a national literature. He was much less an admirer of the great body of Russian Christian writings, sermons, hagiographies and the rest. Since he didn't think Orthodoxy was central to the Russian nation, its writings could not have been a Russian national literature.

The decisive change, he thought, came with Peter the Great, a genius and a world-historical figure more memorable than Napoleon. Peter was cruel and destructive as all dynamic leaders in that early stage of Russian society had to be, but he created a new Russia. Peter brought Europe to Russia, but more importantly, he freed the potential new Russia from its backwardness as Michelangelo said he freed a statue from the marble. In bringing Europe to Russia he did not break or distort Russia's development, but pushed it from its played-out stage of history to a new progressive one whose end was not yet. Peter took the decisive steps to begin the formation of a mature Russian nation, but he could not complete it; that took time and was not quite complete in Belinskii's own day.

Russian literature then, in Belinskii's German Romantic sense of a continuous, integrated, organic national literature, could not have existed before Peter. There was a self-conscious effort to found Russian literature by Prince Antiokh D. Kantemir (1709-1744). But the true founder of what would eventually become a full Russian literature was Mikhail Lomonosov (1711-1765), the peasant from the White Sea who raised himself by force of intellect and character to become the Benjamin Franklin of Russia, a polymath scientist, a cultural politician, the most brilliant member of the Academy of Sciences, the founder of the University of Moscow - and a poet. The golden moment came in 1739, when Lomonosov, studying in Germany, sent back an *Ode on the Taking of Khotin* by the Russian army. Lomonosov, Belinskii thought, had talent but not literary genius. His function in Russian literature, analogous to Peter's in Russian history, was to bring Europe to Russia and thereby make Russia free itself. He brought European genres of poetry, meters and imagery to Russian verse, alien and rhetorical in one aspect, but profoundly liberating in another.

The next stage, growing organically out of Lomonosov's achievement, was dominated by the poet Gavrila R. Derzhavin (1743-1816). Just as Catherine the Great's Russia was was far more developed than that of Lomonosov's youth, so Derzhavin's talent could be greater and more diverse. He was a master of craggy,

43

powerful Russian, much less rhetorical than Lomonosov's, the author of impressive elegies such as *The Death of Prince Meshcherskii* and thundering odes such as *The Waterfall*.

The third stage of the growth of Russian literature was dominated by Nikolai M. Karamzin (1766-1826), who, even more than Lomonosov, adopted a great many French and German words into literary Russian, provoking a bitter controversy with linguistically purist nationalists. Belinskii ridiculed the purists, for he thought a healthy language of a healthy nation could adopt with profit, but he was glad that Pushkin later provided a moderate model of borrowing for literary Russian. Karamzin also adopted from France its version of the sentimental novella in his *Poor Lisa*, and died while writing twelve overpowering volumes of *The History of the Russian State* in the elaborate style of Chateaubriand. Belinskii thought its style splendid for its day, but he disagreed wholly with its glorification of the old and modern Russian monarchy as the creator, sustainer and core of the Russian nation, so contrary to Belinskii's own Herderian ideas about what a nation is, and so reactionary.

And then came the glorious age of Aleksandr Pushkin, one of the two Russian writers (with Gogol) whom Belinskii would call a genius in his full German Romantic sense of the term, a man with the highest possible degree of human creative imagination. But Belinskii, with a splendid lack of chauvinism, ranked Pushkin as less of a genius than his two supreme models, Homer and Shakespeare. This was essentially due to Pushkin's placement in Russia in the years after 1815, when Russia was simply not a mature nation in Belinskii's sense yet. So its greatest poet, even though he wrought miracles and caused Russia to grow several sizes in the process, could not be a Shakespeare.

It was Belinskii in his longest and most sustained work, his eleven articles on Pushkin (1843-44), who canonized him in the eyes of the Russian public as the first truly national Russian poet, as Shakespeare was the English national poet. (Gogol had done so, less thunderingly, a bit earlier). Pushkin was not Classical in spite of his consummate technique and was not a Romantic in spite of his touching tales of tragic love or his self-revelatory personal lyrics. He grew organically out of the achievements of his great predecessors, Karamzin and Vasili A. Zhukovskii (1783-1852) (on whom Belinskii had spilled the wine), a giant standing on the shoulders of very tall men.

Pushkin's works, especially *Evgenii Onegin*, were truly national, reflecting the Russian landscape, seasons, customs, people and spirit. For Belinskii this did *not* mean that Pushkin slopped on local color and *muzhik* dialect in a false effort to be peasanty-national, a technique Belinskii detested. No, his most truly Russian characters were his articulate, Western-educated men and women of the noble class, who could in life move easily in Western society as Pushkin's works could, though they were not yet, easily be comprehended in Europe, a sign of their high quality.

Pushkin's poetry was pure, objective art, by which Belinskii meant the highest praise for technique and beauty, but also an implication of detachment and non-intention to educate and uplift, which Belinskii demanded of the theoretically highest literature, especially future Russian literature. Nonetheless, though not a realist, Pushkin portrayed Russian and general human reality, enabling the Russian public to recognize its national spirit, virtues, and defects, and laying the foundations for a future national effort to transcend the limitations of the Russia of the 1820s.

Not all of Pushkin's works were successes in Belinskii's eyes. He was repelled by the despair and negativity of *The Gypsies*, in which a psychically destroyed young Russian gentleman flees to the gypsies and marries a daughter of nature, but is driven to murder her. His most perfect work, Belinskii felt, was *The Bronze Horseman*, the glorification of the great Peter's great idea and great city. Belinskii maintained that Pushkin's work was practically done by 1830, in spite of his youth, for the phase of un-self-conscious Russian landlord society, which he represented and portrayed, was passing forever, and others of the new age would have to take up the torch. Yet even the immensely more mature, better, greater, future Russia with its immensely broader, higher literature would always look back to Pushkin as the English look back to their Shakespeare.

Belinskii's criticism of Pushkin is much less alien to our sensibility than his criticism of later Russian writers. He provided no formal criticism in our sense, but we, too, find it hard to apply our mechanical techniques of criticism to Pushkin's marble perfection. We are not engaged in the effort to move Nicholas I's Russia as Belinskii was, but we share much of Belinskii's view of Pushkin's relation to the Russia of the 1820s. Much of Belinskii's detailed discussion of Pushkin, as we shall see in Chapter 6, consisted of the analysis of Pushkin's characters as if they were real people and the drawing of lessons from them. We don't do that any more, but what Belinskii did with Pushkin's characters somehow seems much less egregiously old-fashioned than his similar procedures with later writers.

Pushkin's early death ensured that Belinskii could consider him as a whole from the start. He had the inestimable privilege for fourteen years of watching later Russian writers unfold before his eyes, or begin to.

The first and for Belinskii the most important of these writers was Nikolai Gogol. We now read Gogol's stories in anthologies with little regard to the order in which they were written. It is hard to recapture the excitement of the Russian public as successive collections of his stories first appeared, which long remained in their original constellations. The first group was *Evenings on a Farm Near Dikanka*, which came out in 1831 and made Gogol famous overnight. This was before Belinskii began to write, but he was firmly at his post at the *Moscow Telescope* when Gogol's next volumes appeared, and he did his best to do justice to them.

So it is not precise to say that Belinskii discovered Gogol, who emerged without his help. But Belinskii's consistent championship thereafter demonstrably extended Gogol's reputation and helped his sales. More important, Belinskii's glowing reviews deepened the Russian public's conception of Gogol, and perhaps even Gogol's own *Evenings on a Farm Near Dikanka* is hilarious, and was received as a riot of fun, not unlike the enthusiasm for *The Pickwick Papers* in England a few years later. But few thought they were reading a profound artist. That was Belinskii's work; he persuaded the Russian public and thereby the whole world that Gogol's irresistible humor was only the surface layer of works of genius which apprehended and portrayed the serious reality of that age of the Russian nation.

The first Gogol, the author of the stories, was most definitively dealt with by Belinskii in his *On the Russian Story and the Stories of Gogol*, which appeared in the *Moscow Telescope* late in 1835. Gogol, he judged, was a truly great realist, but of quite an unexpected sort. How simple his stories are, how natural and true, but also how new, independent and original! For several theoretical and emotional reasons, Belinskii insisted on Gogol's originality. He scoffed at the idea that Gogol's humor owed anything to Laurence Sterne. (Modern critics think it did). Gogol was not at all an Hoffmannesque fantasist. (Modern critics find a lot of Hoffmann in *The Terrible Vengeance, Viy, The Portrait* and *The Nose*). Actually, Belinskii didn't really like *The Terrible Vengeance* and didn't say much about the other three. He did like *The Diary of a Madman*, which has no sinister Hoffmannesque ambiguity; the anti-hero simply goes mad and is in no way taken over by another world. But Belinskii's favorite was *How Ivan Ivanovich Quarreled with Ivan Nikiforovich*. Belinskii expresses the feelings of a man who still couldn't get over chuckling at the ordinary, everyday, unpretentious, banal yet supremely truthful and revealing quarrel of the two Ivans, best friends until they split forever over the word, "goose". Another favorite was *The Old World Landowners*, who spend their lives eating wholesome country foods and just fade into death. Another was *Nevskii Prospect*, in which Belinskii chiefly admired the ineffective and cowardly mediocrity, Lieutenant Pirogov. These are not satires, he said, but are replete with kindly laughter. Gogol has taken the most humble and everyday current Russian reality and made it poetry. – Clearly, Belinskii was responding only to the happier end of the broad spectrum of signals Gogol was sending out.

The next Gogol, the author of *The Inspector-General*, was often discussed by Gogol, but most ripely four years after the scandal of the play's first performance, in an article in *Notes of the Fatherland* in January 1840. The play and its comedy, he wrote, center on the contrast between the hierarchical worlds of illusion in which the characters move and bumble into each other in a mockery of conflict – and reality, which the audience knows all along, but which appears on stage only at the end with the final messenger. The mayor and the rest of the clumsy scoundrels are completely deluded; Khlestakov presently deludes himself that he is manipulating their delusions; Osip fancies that he is more grounded in reality than his master, Khlestakov, and so on. All of this provides a needed lesson, Belinskii preached, for reality is the affirmation of life but illusion is its negation. The delightful absurdity of the play lies in its faithful representation of the unreality so many Russians live in.

The climactic Gogol was the author of *Dead Souls*, which was of course reviewed by Belinskii when it came out in 1842. *Dead Souls*, he wrote, is Gogol's greatest work, and not just because its length allows sustained treatment of his themes. It no longer deals with the Ukrainian periphery of Russia, but with the heart of the country, geographically and spiritually. It is not, whatever the public may think, such a funny book; everything in it is serious, quiet, true and profound. The Slavophiles were wrong to call it the Russian epic. Epics arise from a much earlier stage of society and exalt national life, but *Dead Souls* examines Russian national life surgically, lays it open and hits it hard. Unlike his earlier comedies in which Gogol had presented reality by negating delusion, here we Russians must see ourselves directly. The lyrical digressions, especially the most famous one about the rushing *troíka* of Russia's national destiny tell us that we must rouse ourselves, and where we have to go.

It is easy to point out Belinskii's very partial comprehension of Gogol. He increasingly assumed that Gogol was what he himself was becoming more and more - a rousing, realist, secular, left critic of Russian society. Gogol certainly permitted and even cultivated that delusion for years, but was becoming less and less so. In 1846 Gogol revealed the intense Christianity and much of the inner agony that had always characterized him. Belinskii rounded on him, in reviews and in his celebrated *Letter to Gogol*, as a sell-out. This, more than anything else in Belinskii's critical career, makes him seem obtuse and proto-Communist to us.

An even more alienating disjunction from Belinskii comes from another set of things he didn't notice in Gogol and presumably couldn't notice: the absurdity - not in Belinskii's comic sense but in our existential sense of the purposeless and meaningless evil in Gogol's portrayals of life in Nicholas I's bureaucratic Russia which prefigure the bureaucratic public side of our lives - and the nightmarish horrors of Gogol's inner soul which spring out from situations in his stories that prefigure the psychotic private side of our lives. Belinskii was a great prophet of the realist vision of the immediate future. He selected that side of Gogol's rich writings to formulate, exemplify and summon up the realist future. The clarity of his short range vision blinded Belinskii to the other sides of Gogol, which turned out to be visions of long enough range to reach our own times.

The years 1837 to 1841 when Belinskii was wrestling restlessly with Fichte's and Hegel's doctrines and then distancing himself from them were also the years of Mikhail Lermontov's meteoric poetic career and early death in a duel. In spite of his own rapidly changing theories, few of which predisposed him toward Lermontov's writings, he hailed and championed this great writer throughout his brief, stormy years on the literary scene.

Lermontov, whose personal situation and death seemed to duplicate Pushkin's, was not a second Pushkin, Belinskii insisted. He was not a genius but a great talent. He was a more troubled and saturnine spirit of this later age, which he expressed better than Pushkin could have. His descriptions of the Romantic Caucasus were not themselves Romantic, Belinskii distinguished, but were

wild and exaggerated recreations of it. Normally Belinskii did not
like that sort of thing, but he was impressed by Lermontov's version
of it.   *Mtsiri*, the story of a daemonic mountain child kidnapped
by civilization but unable to endure it, Belinskii found strange,
powerful and disturbing. *The Demon*, about the hopeless love of a
kind of ultimately alienated Lucifer for a mortal princess, he found
even better. Yet his favorite poem of Lermontov's, and therefore of
the Communists after him, was *The Song of Tsar Ivan Vasilevich, of
the Young Oprichnik and of the Valiant Merchant Kalashnikov*, a
latter day heroic ballad in which the merchant saves his life through
strength, skill and wit in the murderous court of Ivan the Terrible.

      The great problem for critics of Lermontov at that time was
his novel, or collection of five tales, *A Hero of Our Time*.
Belinskii rejected the idea that its hero, Pechorin - a womanizing,
dueling, emotionally burnt out young Russian officer - was Byronic;
he was peculiarly modern, 1840-ish. Belinskii detailed the ways in
which Pechorin differed from Onegin. He was not only more brutal
and sinister but, more importantly, he was more internally dis-
integrated, reflecting the rapid breakup of one era and the formation of another at that moment. Precisely because Pechorin truly
reflected the tumultuous reality of the day Belinskii fought to
free him of the conventional charge that he was a villain whose semi-
sympathetic treatment by Lermontov corrupted readers. Truth will
benefit us, Belinskii was sure, though perhaps in a sequel Lermontov
might find a way to make Pechorin or an equivalent character more
positive.

      Precisely because Belinskii did not impose his own shifting
ideology of those years too strictly on Lermontov's works, because
he admitted simultaneous puzzlement at and powerful attraction to
Lermontov, we find his criticism of Lermontov rather attractive.

      The next giant on the traditional list of Belinskii's dis-
coveries was actually the first obscure and diffident young man
whom he truly discovered and championed at the moment of discovery,
making all the difference at the diffident beginning of a career
that would later become truly great - Ivan Turgenev. The work which
Belinskii hailed was the manuscript of his early narrative-
psychological poem, *Parasha*, in 1843. Belinskii was polite about
the verse but saved his enthusiasm for the psychological truthfulness of the portrait of the woman. What he was saying was that
Turgenev was good at what could be well done in prose, a prescient
guess.

      Belinskii continued to encourage Turgenev, now his friend, in
his abortive career as a poet, but he lived just long enough to
read *Khor and Kalinych* and three other stories from the series he
would never see finished, *A Sportsman's Sketches*, Turgenev's first
major prose work and first masterpiece. Belinskii hailed them as
works of real talent, but with the qualification that Turgenev's
talent lay in recording the reality he saw exactly, not in the
higher sphere of creating reality out of the raw material he saw.
This was not such a silly statement about these stories, and the
diffident Turgenev often judged himself, ruefully, in the same way.
But once again we cannot help feeling that Belinskii brilliantly
recognized a young writer he had called forth but blindly failed

to grasp the true nature and extent of his genius.

Chronologically, Belinskii's last great discovery was Ivan Goncharov (1812-1891), who published his first novel, *An Ordinary Story*, in 1847. Once more Belinskii hailed a new talent, recognized the novel's qualities, – but didn't really warm to it. It was a work of pure art, not of passion or engagement. The author was detached from his quite imperfect characters; readers might take them or leave them. What was magnificently appropriate to his time in Pushkin was not in the spirit of the times and a bit repellent in 1847, though skillfully done. We feel that Belinskii's political-ethical ideas were partly, but only very partially, overbalancing his judgment.

But it is traditional to say that Belinskii's last great discovery was Dostoevskii. Annenkov caught Belinskii in the very act. *Poor Folk* was the first example in ·Russia of the "social novel", which, following his critical theory, he had predicted would come to be, express and characterize the coming age. He found it a detailed, convincing and compassionate account of how life in Russia grinds two decent little people down, which could not fail to have some social effect.

He had predicted and called for it, and here it came, but with a craggy artistic power that was almost too much to hope for, a better social novel in his judgment that those of Eugène Sue or George Sand. *Poor Folk* was ten per cent too long and sometimes repetitious, but these were the youthful faults of a superabundant talent and gave great promise for the future.

But the future, as it began to come, distressed Belinskii. *The Double,* he thought, had many splendid parts suitable to the social novel it should have been. But the central, fantastic character, the doubled Goliadkin, and the central situation – was he mad from the start or driven mad by supernatural intervention? – struck Belinskii as all wrong, just the sort of recidivism to Hoffmann which the novel, as a genre, did not need. And two stories, the only other works of Dostoevskii he was to live to read, he thought even worse and more perverse.

Then death took Belinskii before he could see what Dostoevskii would develop into. We are left with violently conflicting sentiments. For the dying Belinskii to recognize and champion the unknown Dostoevskii strikes us as the deeply moving inspiration of genius. But then we become convinced that Belinskii recognized only the fact of the talent, nothing of the nature of it. We see Belinskii disliking Dostoevskii's work as it becomes more and more what we know to be Dostoevskian. We have that sinking feeling that had Belinskii lived, he would have hated *The Brothers Karamazov*. We shall never know.

Scholars and students alike find it very difficult to make up their minds about Belinskii's critical position and career. His German Romantic theories of life, literature and criticism, even when examined with willed sympathy, even when it is granted that he and Herder *did* what their theories said they should do, are simply too monist and uniformitarian, too prescriptive in their notions of what the world is like and how literature should describe it, to appeal to us.

If Belinskii worked such theories to call forth the Russian realist novel, which we admire infinitely more, it seems another example of the greatest historical mystery: how does a lesser engender a greater? He must have done it, but did he more than half understand what he was doing? In the whole corpus of his writings, we say, there isn't one example of even college-level analysis of an actual text. If Belinskii's closest literary followers today are the Communists, it confirms us in our rejection. He could not pull off his trick again. - And yet, do we actually have the arrogance to claim that we know better than Turgenev's judgment of what he knew and loved best? Something must have been at work in Belinskii which escapes us even after prolonged study. The complicated task of outlining Belinskii's critical position is far easier than the task of formulating our critical position on him.

CHAPTER   5

"LITERARY REVERIES"

BELINSKII'S first major work, with which he burst upon and captured the world of the newborn Russian *intelligentsia*, was his *Literary Reveries*, an extended essay on Russian literature, Russian nationhood and a very great deal else. It was published in ten issues of the *Report*, the weekly supplement of the *Moscow Telescope*, from September through December 1834, a period in which its editor, Nikolai Nadezhdin, had left Belinskii in charge of his thick journal. It runs to about 100 pages in modern editions.

To modern Russians it is an historic and deeply moving classic. To modern Westerners it is a curious production, a mixed bag. There is little or nothing in it that a fashionable modern professor of literature would admit as literary criticism at all. It is regarded by most of the few Westerners who have read it as a sweepingly assertive congeries of rhetorical opinions, Romantic in the worst sense: bombastic, vapid and incoherent.

The very serious and sympathetic scholar of Belinskii, Herbert Bowman, wrote, "The *Reveries* present a diffuse panorama of literary history and aesthetic doctrine; ... The striking feature of the *Reveries* ... is their disjointedness. The piecemeal manner of composition and publication could only have aggravated that fault; yet some of the most abrupt movements in the writing appear within a single short installment ... The *Reveries* appear to contain nothing original but to constitute a disorderly passing-in-review of critical propositions widely shared ... The title of the *Reveries* itself suggests their illogical structure and irregular pace; it may also suggest their brokenness of theme ..." (1).

The distinguished historian of Russia, Geroid Tanquary Robinson, was less kind. In class he would say, "Belinskii's *Literary Reveries* was a double disaster for Russia, in itself for its gassy dogmas and miserable writing and for the future revolutionaries and Communists who were inspired by Belinskii to freeze that kind of sweeping nonsense and that kind of wretchedly bad style into the Party line" (2).

It is the major thesis of this book that Belinskii deserves better of us than this. He was not an aristocrat and he neither strove for nor achieved that apparently effortless ease, lightness and grace of the writing of the French Eighteenth Century, or of Pushkin or Griboedov. His writing did not have the virtue which the Greeks called *charitas*. On the other hand, as America's foremost scholar of Russian thought, George Kline, maintains, Belinskii's writing is always interesting and powerful.

And it is certainly Romantic. We are most sympathetic to the aims and procedures of the great Romantic artists in the realm of music. We understand their principled disregard of form, logic and rules. We glory with them in their *illogical structures* and their *irregular pace,* in their *abrupt movements* and their *brokenness of theme.* We are stirred with them by their startling changes of volume, rhythm, tone color and mood. We remember the many Romantic pieces entitled *Reveries* precisely in order to intimate the freely associative, shifting, Kaleidoscopic music they contain. We connect this kind of music above all with the name of Franz Liszt, born like Belinskii in the year 1811. Romantics in all fields hoped to break through what they called the superficial, arid, rationalist logic-chopping of French Classicism to plunge, with "the illogic of Shakespeare", into the real depths of the life of nations and of the human heart.

The unmusical Belinskii was not directly imitating Romantic musical forms. But if we approach his *Literary Reveries* and his other major works in the frame of mind we adopt when about to listen to Romantic music, if we are receptive to the apparent disorder of words and ideas that may be the unconscious order of real life, to the apparent illogic that may be the external expression of profound truth, we may find ourselves responding to some hitherto unapprecia-ted master-works of Romantic art.

*   *   *

Literary Reveries (Literaturnye Mechtaniia) it is called, *An Elegy in Prose.* The very title contains at least two ironies: a Romantic reverie both is and is not a structureless, pointless dream, and the elegy – the reader does not yet know for what – will turn out to be both a lament for the non-existence of Russian literature and its opposite. A reader in 1834 knew the dual sense in which "reverie" was then used, and he would be led to suspect further ironies. Irony was a prominent Romantic mode; completely compatible with high-serious goals.

The first of the ten installments, like all the rest, has comic-serious quotations at the head of it to sound some of the themes. The first is three lines from Griboedov's *Woe from Wit,* beginning, "I'll tell you such truth that's worse than any lie" (3). This was first of all a plain statement of Belinskii's view and intentions. But *Woe from Wit* is the great Russian counterpart of Molière's *Le misanthrope,* and the speaker, Chatskii, is the Russian Alceste, who tells plain truths with such unrestrained, daemonic forcefulness that his friends are repelled rather than enlightened, leading to his own discomfiture. In comparing himself to

Chatskii, Belinskii was both twitting and exhorting his readers, and probably expressing a private doubt about his own character and fate. The second quotation is from "Baron Brambeus", the pseudonym of a humorist Belinskii usually despised: "'Do you have good books?' 'No, but we have great writers'. 'Then at least you have a literature?' 'On the contrary, we only have a book trade'"(4). - which thumbnails the goofy pretentiousness that Belinskii was about to attribute to the Russian literary scene.

The actual text begins with a breathy mock-elegy for Russian literature: "Do you remember that blessed time when our literature was awakened by a breath of life, when talent after talent appeared, poem after poem ... that splendid time when we were firmly convinced ... that we had our own Byrons, Shakespeares, Schillers and Walter Scotts? Alas! Where art thou, *o bon vieux temps* ..." (5) and so on in the mode that Belinskii was to discover in Gogol: farcing everything up in order to reveal what lies too deep for tears.

There follows a kind of laundry list of then living Russian writers, starting with Pushkin who "in powerful and stirring songs first smelled the breath of Russian life", but who had now strangely fallen silent, but descending abruptly to the third through twentieth rate writers whom he merely named in the plural, "the Greches and Kalashnikovs ..." in order to deny them immortality. And finally, "What are the causes of such a void in our litersture?" followed by a question that continues the mockery and also suggests a sudden seriousness, "Or is it really the case that *we have no literature*?" (6) And that is all there is to the first installment: a farce, some unease and the first sounding of some themes that will be developed tremendously.

Naturally, the second installment begins with a *fortissimo* playing of the main theme, "Yes - we have no literature!" (7) by massed brasses. Then a full stop, and a resumption of the cackling farce with the piccolos and Chinese gongs: "I hear thousands of voices in answer to my rude sally" squawking that Russia does too have a literature. Belinskii alleges to answer, in an hilarious sentence more than 500 words long, composed of clauses such as, "in spite of the fact that our young lion of poetry, our mighty Kukolnik, has at his first leap overtaken the universal genius of Goethe ..." and ending with, "in spite of all this, I repeat, *we have no literature*! - Oof! I'm tired!" (8).

What has Belinskii gained from this *buffo* introduction? A perceptive reader could feel the air cleared. Through a temporary excess of farce, he has been induced to hunger for the sober discussion that is to follow, which might not have been so attractive if entered on cold. Like Gogol, who was at that time writing his best stories, Belinskii felt that the colossal complacency of so much of Russia was best attacked with sledgehammer mockery, which stood the best chance of inducing the most elementary self-recognition of defect.

Well then, what *is* a literature? Not the sum of all writing in a country and not just an assemblage of masterpieces.

"... a literature is the collection of the artistic verbal productions born of free inspiration ... of people created for art ... fully expressing and recreating in their polished creations the spirit of the people amid whom they were born and brought up, whose life they live and whose spirit they breathe, expressing in their creative works its inner life down to its hidden depths and pulsation" (9). Such a literature must evolve smoothly and organically, without any breaks or leaps caused by outside influences.

This was not an everyday definition of literature then or now. It was Belinskii's first public statement of his ideas about literature which he had absorbed from his study of the German Romantics in Stankevich's circle. There were three operative factors here: a genuine literature must be *free*, *popular* and *national*, all of which had political implications in Nicholas's Russia.

Belinskii does not protract this solemn movement. He shifts to three pages of farcical *bravura* passages about what he is *not* about to do, and then returns to literature. A literature is the expression of a nation and it will vary in each country. French literature expresses beautifully and admirably the elegance of the *beau monde*, Italian literature love and art, English literature practical affairs, German literature the learning and philosophy that is the inner life of the whole German people and Russian literature ... (10).

But on the verge of this climax Belinskii breaks off the orchestra's music and launches it suddenly into a sustained, lyric, rhapsodic movement, the poetic climax of the whole composition, ostensibly on the nature of art as a whole.

"The whole infinite, beautiful, divine world is nothing but the breath of a single, eternal *idea* (the idea of one eternal God) manifesting itself in innumerable forms, as a great spectacle of absolute unity in endless diversity" (11). "How great is the *body* of this soul of the universe, the heart of which is formed by gigantic suns, its arteries by Milky Ways, its blood by pure ether" (12). "The wheel of time goes round at the highest speed; in the boundless skies lights go out like extinct volcanoes and new ones blaze up ..." (13). And likewise the continuous birth and destruction of all things on earth and in human societies. "What then is the purpose and aim of art? - *To portray, to recreate in words, sounds, line and colors the idea of the universal life of nature*" (14).

Of all artists, only "Shakespeare, the divine, the great, the unequaled Shakespeare, understood hell and earth and heaven; the tsar of nature, he exacted equal tribute from good and evil, and saw, in his inspired clairvoyance, the beating pulse of the universe!" (15). "Did not one and the same divine spirit make the gentle lamb and the bloodthirsty tiger, the graceful horse and the deformed whale ! the beautiful Circassian maid and the hideous Negro?" (16) !   "Yes - *art is the expression of the great idea of the universe in its endless diversity of appearances!*" (17) And so on, to the end of the third installment.

To Belinskii's contemporaries, this was the magnificent climax of a tremendous piece of poetry and music. We can study and understand the German Romantic ideas, feelings and phrases which Belinskii was recreating in Russia, but they no longer have the power to stir us. This whole rhapsodic movement was inserted in Belinskii's sequence of discussions of nationalities, just before the last and greatest. For a Russian, there could be only one climax that would overtop even universal heaven, even this poetically pantheist and quite un-Orthodox God, and that was Russia itself.

And so the fourth installment, less rhapsodic but more weighty music, is the intellectual climax of the work, the discussion of nationhood and Russian nationality. This lyricism about unity and diversity turns out to have a distinct nationalist point: Russia, however huge, is not the universe. It is one nation among many. Its contribution comes from being special, not from being what other nations are. And those passages about the greatest spirit, the truest artist comprehending the whole of nature, including the ugly and the evil - the lesson for any Russian writer (such as Gogol) would be clear, for in Russia he would have so *very* much of this material to work with.

"And so, now we have to decide the following question: what is our literature: the expression of society or the expression of the national spirit? The resolution of this question will be the history of our literature ..." (18). Belinskii would undertake that history from the fifth installment on. This fourth installment deals with nationhood and Russian nationhood in general. In these abstract discussions, the Russian word for "nation" is *narod*, whose primary meaning is "people", and which is often used to mean "people" as opposed to government. But Belinskii and the other Nineteenth Century Russians never contrasted "people" to "nation"; *narod*, strictly, should be translated as "nation-people" or "people who constitute a nation", but "nation" is traditionally and justifiably used by Russian and foreign translators alike.

"Every nation, following the inexorable law of Providence, must express in its life some side of the life of the whole of humanity; if not, that people does not live but vegetates ..." (19). Few of us would agree, but think of the advantages to a nationalist if this were true, the possibilities for members of depressed, humiliated nations to construct a theoretical ground for renewed self-esteem.

"Onesidedness is bad for each individual and especially bad for all of humanity. When the whole world became Rome, when all nations began to think and feel like Romans, then the progress of the human mind was interrupted" (20). This was a splended justification for the nationalism of all nations not at the head of the procession, not ancient Rome, not modern France and Western Europe.

"Wherein lies the originality of each nation? It consists of a special cast of mind and way of looking at things, in a religion, language and especially *customs* ... all originate in one common source - the primary cause - *climate* and *location*. Among the distinguishing traits of each nation *customs* play the most important role ... It is impossible to imagine a nation without religious concepts embodied in forms of worshipping God; it is impossible to imagine a nation that does not have one single language for all classes [Stalin would quote this last] ; still less is it possible to imagine a nation not having its own characteristic customs. These customs consist of the forms of dress, which are explained by the country's climate; in forms of domestic and social life whose causes lie in the nation's creed, superstitions and beliefs ... They are the physiognomy of a nation and without them a nation is a form without a face ... The younger a nation, the more striking and colorful are its customs, and the greater is the importance it places on them ... Destroy its customs suddenly without replacing them with new ones ... and you annihilate the nation ... Any nation can borrow from another, but it has to place the stamp of its own genius on these *borrowings* ..." (21).

Naturally, in this abstract discussion of nationhood, we can see that Belinskii's model was the Russian nation, with its notably extreme climate, its prized language that had been the subject of such heated debate, its striking customs so beloved in the Romantic age, its alleged youth as opposed to Europe, its famous borrowings from the West. Religion is also in Belinskii's list. Perhaps he was less anticlerical in 1834 than in the 1840s when he wrote his *Letter to Gogol*. Perhaps, as the Communists suggest, this was a bow to the censor. We notice that "creed" is followed by "superstitions", not a very pious touch.

In fact, the whole passage is much less like Burke, Karamzin and the conservative Romantics than it first appears to be. The emotion-laden peculiarities of the Russian nation are alleged to have been caused by the Enlightened Montesquieu's explanatory factors, climate and location. The talk of young nations borrowing with profit and without giving up their identity was a common line of argument then in favor of reforming Russia. And then we notice the thundering absence of any mention of Russia's most famous peculiar institution, serfdom ...

After so much discussion of Russia under the guise of abstraction, Belinskii can now throw off the pretense: "To the east of Europe, on the border of two parts of the world, Providence has settled a nation differing sharply from its western neighbors" (22). There follows a cadenza on the history of Russia, beginning with apparent traditional loyalty: "It stood stoutly for the church of God, for the faith of its forefathers, and was unyieldingly true to the little father, the Orthodox tsar" (23). When he comes to the westernization of Peter the Great, Belinskii's tone became both grander - "He was one of those giants who lifted the terrestrial globe on his shoulders" (24). - and more *brio* - "Farewell, thou simple and noble clipped hair at the crown, which went so well with these venerable beards! Thou hast been replaced by gigantic periwigs, sprinkled with flour!" (25).

And so Russia split in two. "The mass of the nation stubbornly remained what it was, but society proceeded along the path on which the mighty hand of a genius had set it" (26). On this subject Belinskii's ideas differed significantly from his German Romantic model. German society in the Eighteenth Century did not differ from French anywhere near so much as Russia's had differed from Europe.

Herder thought the invasion of French fashions in manners and culture was degrading the upper stratum of a basically sound society, and should be thrown back. Belinskii thought that Peter's westernization split the Russian people existentially into a miserable, enserfed mass with its moving but horrendously backward (and in Belinskii's German sense *unformed*) customs, and a state-directed nobility that was moving Russia along the proper path of progress, in spite of its many excesses and foibles in imitating the West. Censorship kept him from a full statement of his views here, but they were clearly indicated.

After all this sweep and energy, Belinskii lets his fourth section fall away toward the end into a farcical promise that he would at last undertake his history of Russian literature. He does so starting in the fifth installment: "With Lomonosov our literature begins; he was its father and guide; he was its Peter the Great"(27). This sovereign assertion that Russian literature *is* modern, westernized Russian literature is made even more magisterial by his total omission of any mention here of the opposite view which every reader would be thinking of, that Russian literature had begun in Kiev 900 years earlier.

Not until three installments later does Belinskii bother to counter the normal view, and then only in an insulting footnote: "Our literature, without any doubt, began in 1739 when Lomonosov sent from abroad his first ode, *On the Taking of Khotin* ... Do we have to prove that *The Tale of the Host of Igor, The Tale of the Battle on the Don,* the eloquent *Epistle of Vassian to Ivan III* and various historical records, folk songs and scholastic spiritual rhetoric have only as much relationship to our literature as the records of antediluvian literature would have had, if they had been discovered, to *Sanskrit, Greek* or *Latin* literature?" (28).

We can recall the tenets of German Romantic theory into which this view of Belinskii's fit,but it still seems a bit perverse to us. To Russians in 1834, this total discounting of the cultural achievements of Old Russia was not a piece of German intellection but a resounding radical blast, perverse indeed to convervatives but a stirring call to the *intelligentsia*. If Old Russian literature was ruled out, then by definition modern, westernized Russian literature could not yet have been the *continuous, integrated* voice of the *whole* nation that Belinskii's theory required any true literature to be, and then yes, we have no literature.

But this was not just a definitional exercise. Belinskii had not defined Russian nationhood by the same standard, as he might have, and had not claimed that Old Russia was dead, the new Russia as yet unformed and yes, we have no nation. Peter had split the Russian nation; there was and is a nation to be split and bound together. With inspired Romantic inconsistency, Belinskii had defined the nation in one way so as to have it and literature in another way so as not to have it. Since the nation was there, the *purpose* of literature was there: to express, exalt and press forward the national spirit. But since the literature was not yet fully formed, the most intense ethical-national effort was required to call it into being - and so Belinskii's heart's desires in both the

57

present and the future were interlinkedly served.

The fifth through the ninth installments, half the number of the series and far more than half its total length, are devoted to the history of what Belinskii has thus narrowly defined as Russian literature. Then and now, an informed reader would learn nothing about Lomonosov, Derzhavin, Fonvizin, Karamzin or Pushkin from these articles. Then and now, they are read to discover Belinskii's judgments on all these writers and on everything else he judges, mostly on the national theme.

Belinskii's judgments are ambivalent and paradoxical throughout. Each historical period of Russian (semi-)literature seems to be introduced with a traditional, loyal paean of praise to the monarch of the time. "Catherine II became the monarch and an era of new, better life began for the Russian nation ..." (29). "The age of Alexander the Beneficent belongs in the brightest period of the life of the Russian nation ..." (30). Communists interpret such passages as excusable lies to get by the censors in the darkest age of Nicholas I. Cold War Western scholars have cited them as proof that the vauntedly radical Belinskii was an unthinking monarchist for most of his career.

If one reads the censored text, as one must, with as sharp an ear for what is not said as an eye for what is printed, one notices that the tsars praised are Peter, Catherine and Alexander, and that they are praised for genuine progressive achievements, such as Alexander's promotion of education. Belinskii does not praise them for all of their policies, certainly not for maintaining and strengthening serfdom. There is no mention of Anna, Elizabeth, Peter III or Paul. And then one notices the screaming silence about Nicholas. Belinskii has managed to get past the censor his praise for the enlightened despots of the past, exclusively for their progressive acts and tendencies which in the 1830s were the program of Russian liberals in opposition to Nicholas's police state. Russian readers were rather skilled at figuring such things out.

The enlightened despots were sincerely praised for providing the setting and stimulus for Russian literature. The Age of Lomonosov was prolonged by Catherine II's intelligent promotion throughout her reign, ornamented by the dramatist Fonvizin and the poet Derzhavin – to whom Belinskii would in later works grant an "Age" of his own. And Alexander I stimulated and presided over the next period, the Age of Karamzin, and made possible the launching of the greatest period yet, the Age of Pushkin in the 1820s. These were, in Belinskii's judgment, rich periods in Russian literature, especially the last.

And yet ... we remember that Belinskii had started by proclaiming that yes, we have no literature. All this was a second best literature, which could not because of the split in the Russian nation be based soundly and solidly on the people, as German literature was in the same period. It was a brilliant but febrile product of social and cultural schism, a dazzling dance over a volcanic chasm. The very language of this literature drifted away from the speech of the common people, as Russian authors assimilated foreign words and modes of speech.

Belinskii was making a tragic, ambivalent judgment. He was
not saying that these Russian authors were *babus* in British India
jingling away hackishly in half-learned foreign tongues on miscom-
prehended foreign themes. They were great writers who really knew
European culture and literature.   They achieved miracles in assimi-
lating so many foreign ideas to the Russian character and in
naturalizing so many foreign literary modes in the Russian language.
Their great works are excellent in themselves and have much to move
and teach *society*, the Russian upper class, for which they were
written. But they were not based on the mass of the Russian people
and could not be read by them. Therefore they could not fulfill the
highest mission of a literature by Belinskii's German Romantic standards and they did not in the last analysis (as in his first) constitute a truly *Russian* literature. The proof of all this,
Belinskii would maintain at the end of his work, was that this
grand but artificial literature, not sustained by any real roots in
the nation, could not last, and had in fact collapsed in Belinskii's
own day.

At this point Belinskii made his bow to Ivan Krylov (1769-
1844), the antithesis of Karamzin in the latter's own Age. Krylov's
volumes of earthy animal and peasant fables, appearing from 1809 on,
were not quite written in peasant dialect, but gave that impression
when contrasted to the ponderous periods of Karamzin's histories.
And Krylov certainly expressed peasant wit and skepticism about the
order of the world, while Belinskii did not need to state that
Karamzin, in politics, was best known for his memorial to Alexander
I maintaining that serfdom was a marvelous institution while constitutional government would be an horrible disaster for Russia.
Krylov, Belinskii judged, was the nearest approach yet to an authentic national Russian literature.

But readers then and now are most interested in Belinskii's
views of Pushkin. He tackles the already famous distinction between
Classicism and Romanticism. He tweakingly defines Classicism a
"literary Catholicism", meaning not the religion but an authoritarian régime in literature, and more seriously as the devotion to form
over idea, culture over nature, tradition over innovation and the
dead hand of antiquity (31). But "in Russia classicism was neither
more nor less than a faint echo of the European echo" (32).
(Belinskii used an elegant verbal trick in this sentence: the first,
Russian "echo" is the native word "*otgolosok*"; the second, European
"echo" is the European loan-word, "*ekho*").   On the other hand,
"... romanticism was nothing other than a return to naturalness in
art and consequently to originality and nationality, an emphasis on
idea over form and a rejection of the alien and constricting forms
of antiquity ..." (33). It is clear whose side we should be on.
"Pushkin was not strained, he was always truthful and sincere, he
created his own forms for his own ideas; that was his
romanticism" (34).

In later works, Belinskii was to define Romanticism more
narrowly and to maintain that Pushkin was neither Classical nor
Romantic, but here the reverberating word is used to praise
Pushkin's bold forthrightness in Tsarist Russia where it was so rare.

Belinskii alleges inability to judge so great a poetic soul as Pushkin, and indeed he gives brief praise rather than long analysis. "... how quickly and rapidly the Pushkin period proceeded. We can say that life appeared in our literature only in the last decade, and what life! Disturbing, bubbling, active! Life is action, action is struggle, and then we struggled and fought a life-and-death fight" (35). Belinskii, in affirming his basic vitalist aesthetic and ethic, went on to praise the fierce journalistic polemics of Pushkin and his contemporaries, which he himself would revive and surpass. He discusses the other major figures of the decade of the 1820s, especially the dramatist Griboedov who had been murdered by an Iranian mob in Teheran five years before. This was the occasion for another of the intense, lyrical section of this work, a rhapsody to the theatre, which reveals a close reading of Pushkin's rhapsody on the same subject in Chapter One of *Evgenii Onegin*.

After these discussions Belinskii is able to conclude his five installment history of Russian literature. "The Pushkin period was the brightest time in our literature ... We can say positively that then we had, if not a literature, then at least a phantasm of a literature; for then it had movement in it, life and even a kind of continuity and development" (36). This is all but a formal admission that Belinskii's assertion that Russia had no literature was not meant in any literal, historical way. His language in discussing Pushkin and Griboedov is not conditional. He does not mention any gap between their works and the mass of the people (although he was right earlier; these great poets were then unknown to the peasantry). On the contrary, Belinskii's sentences state or imply linkages between Pushkin, his time and the Russian nation.

Is Belinskii's argument then broken, bad from the start? In making it seem so, Belinskii has achieved two things. He created his own form for his own idea of the greatness of Pushkin and his contemporaries: how great Pushkin must be if I am compelled to abandon my own argument before him! And by letting the flame of his argument burn so low at the end of the ninth installment, he has arranged for us to be bowled over by its powerful resurgence in the tenth and last.

Each of the ten installments has a quotation or two in front of it, usually as introductory, rollicking grace notes. Belinskii carries on a running gag about the length of his work, teasing himself for running on and his readers for philistine impatience. Thus the ninth installment is labeled "Next to the last", and the quotation reads, "The shore! The shore!" But the last article is labeled "The conclusion follows", and the quotation, worthy of such an honored place, is from Pushkin, "Still one last tale/And my annals are ended". At first reading this too might seem a goofy quotation, selected for its inappropriate solemnity, another self-mockery. But to Russians these are reverberating words, from *Boris Godunov*, spoken to begin the fifth scene by the holy monk Pimen, who is about to end his monumental chronicle of the works of God and the Devil in Holy Russia with an account of the murder of Dmitri, the one true heir to the Tsardom, by the henchmen of Boris Godunov, a horrible sin which ends the 700-year-old line of

Russian princes and brings on the Time of Troubles. The joke thereby turns solemn, and Belinskii/Pimen has prepared us for the final chapter on the death of Dmitri/Russian literature, and will soon make it clear who the current Boris Godunov is.

"1830, the *cholera* year, was truly the *black* year for our literature, a truly fatal epoch ... there was a kind of violent break. Such unnatural jumps are ... the best proof that we have no literature ... And so the year 1830 ended or rather broke off the *Pushkin* period, for Pushkin himself ended, and with him his influence; and from that time almost no familiar note has been sounded by his lyre ... The journals all died, perhaps from an apoplectic stroke, or actually from the cholera morbus" (37).

The passage begins and ends with the image of cholera, which was an horribly real plague in Russia in 1830-31, which shed great discredit on the government for its initial inefficient response and callous indifference. Why the break? The great figure was Pushkin, who had been only thirty one in 1830, but Belinskii refers to him only in past tenses in these passages. The crises of his art and marriage, which led him to write and publish less and differently after 1830, were not yet well known in 1834, but the rumors of his petty persecutions by court circles had spread widely, and the tolerance of these persecutions by Nicholas himself. Nicholas had come to the throne over the bodies of the Decembrists. He had crushed the Polish rebellion of 1830-31, at the same time ordering a harsher wave of censorship against liberals and their journals in Russia itself. He was thereafter referred to by the young revolutionaries as "Old Cholera". Belinskii was not saying that Nicholas was the sole cause of the "death" of Russian literature, but he certainly believed the Tsar was a major factor in its crisis, and here, with skill and daring, he was saying so.

"And so a new period in our literature began. Who was its head ...? Alas! No one!" (38). Belinskii devotes most of this installment to various unimpressive claimants to Pushkin's mantle. Far more than the readers of 1834, we are struck with the brief, most optimistic paragraph in the survey: "Mr. Gogol, amiably disguised as the *Beekeeper*, presents a number of unusual talents. Who does not know his *Evenings on a Farm Near Dikanka?* How much wit, jollity, poetry and nationality there is in it. God grant that he fully justifies the gifts of which he gives hope!" (39).

But meanwhile, every scribbler affected nationality in his writing, and therefore failed to achieve it, for a truly national writer such as Krylov, Belinskii thought, had to be unconsciously national. Still, the intense study during the 1830s of the Russian past and of the life of the Russian people was something promising to build on. The possible future national literature would have to deal with Russian life. *"The Prisoner of the Caucasus, The Fountain of Bakhchisarai* and *The Gypsies* could have been written by any European poet, but *Evgenii Onegin* and *Boris Godunov* could only have been written by a Russian poet. *Total* nationality can only be achieved by people free of irrelevant foreign influence ... Thus, *our nationality consists of the faithful representation of scenes from Russian life"* (40).

There follow a few pages of mockery of Baron Brambeus, the unsparkling humorist, and his brethren, and then the last ringing climax; "And so, we need not a literature, which will appear in its own good time without any effort on our side, but education!" (41). Earlier, when he wanted to arouse readers, Belinskii had written as if the rebirth/birth of Russian literature were contingent on concerted human effort, and doubtful. Here he invokes (before his knowledge of Hegel) the German Romantic belief in the inevitable, unconscious workings of history to assure us that the literature will come.

The education that is then specifically referred to, in unexpectedly fawning terms, was the campaign of Count Sergei Uvarov, Nicholas's reactionary Minister of Public Instruction, to promote Orthodoxy, Autocracy and Nationality in the schools. Communists hold that this passage was either an utterly insincere bow to the censor on Belinskii's part or (better yet) on the part of Nadezhdin, who had by now, December, 1834, returned to Moscow. Either way, it was clear to most of Belinskii's readers that that was *not* the education he meant. Equally clearly, his enthusiasm expressed several times in this work for the aggressive thick journals and their essential role in promoting literature and forming a unified national spirit can be remembered to supply the missing element. Passionate, enlightened crusading in the thick journals might educate Russia and recreate/create it. This was Belinskii's later explicit conviction, based both on German Romantic theory and on what he knew he was in fact doing. The idea was at least dawning here:

"Yes, at this very time the seed of the future is ripening!... And then we shall have our own literature, we shall be not the imitators but the rivals of the Europeans" (42).

But the last climax is not the end, which displays another formal invention of the Romantics, the falling action, the dying away. The actual last page is another apparent self-deprecation: " ... don't look for a strictly logical order in my elegy in prose. Elegists are never distinguished by great accuracy of reasoning. I intended to set forth several truths, some already known, some my own reflections, but I didn't have enough time to meditate on and polish my article ..." (43).

Most Western scholars who read these words take them at face value. But Russians at the time might have detected three ironical levels of meaning: on the surface, a rational apology for the defects of the work; below the surface, a mocking Romantic assertion of the superiority of the great illogic of life; in the depths, a quite rational Romantic indication to those who could perceive it of the measured, concealed, dissenting argument Belinskii was making.

There is one more ironical pun at the very end: "And so, dear reader, let me wish you a happy new year and new good fortune. Farewell!" (44). This supplement was sent out in December, 1834, but who thought the calendar year 1835 was the only new epoch Belinskii was welcoming?

*   *   *

I hope that Belinskii now seems to be a less sloppy and incoherent writer than has hitherto been thought in the West. He was not insincere in his modest statements. He *was* always rushed and he had a journalist's deadline psychology and rhythm of work. He wrote these *Reveries* in ten installments and was stuck with the earlier ones in print as he wrote the later ones. This is not the highly polished work it might ideally have been. But that is quite different from the charge of rambling disjointedness. The fluid structure of a Romantic composition is not the same thing as gassy incoherence.

As a Romantic, Belinskii believed in unconscious creative forces, and he did compose passages in the heat of the moment. But these were the impulses of a disciplined mind that had determined in advance what the main points and the main roads to them were to be. The sequences and proportions of the teasing passages and the serious ones vary too exactly in accordance with the moods Belinskii wanted to induce to have been accidents. The abrupt switches from straightforward exposition to lyrical rhapsody, and the direction of the flights of the rhapsodies conduce too carefully to the fulfillment of the plan to have been unconscious. Many sorts of music are found in these *Reveries* in all sorts of parallels and contrasts, but there are no inconsistent tones or false notes - save for a few which may not have been written by Belinskii and were certainly written for the censor. Think how very different, how very much finer, Belinskii's kaleidoscopic gloom and mania, argument and illogic, jollity and passion in these *Reveries* are than my exposition of his same critical ideas in the previous chapter. If the passion no longer moves us, at least the wit, as Turgenev said, hits its objects not on the eyebrow but in the eye. Belinskii's *Literary Reveries* was his first consummate work of Romantic art.

But in this genre of writing, art is supposed to be the means to the ends of persuasion and enlightenment. We have no historical doubt that the work *was* persuasive and that it did make Belinskii's reputation and his career. We recognize that Belinskii crystalized a set of German Romantic ideas and his own application of them to Russia for his public here, an important intellectual achievement. But ultimately we judge such works by our opinion of the validity of its ideas. Practically all of us are for Belinskii and freedom and against Nicholas and tyranny, but our approval of his fighting the good fight does not carry over into assent to, much less enthusiasm for, his ideas.

Argument is irrelevant. The original Romantic climate of opinion has passed away forever. Not only our opinions but the structure of our thinking are later and different. It is terribly easy for us to go on from a recognition of that great historical change to a judgment that the ideas of Belinskii's age were false, naive and meaningless, and a contempt for Belinskii's thought. It might be well to remember that if Belinskii's mind does not impress us, it did impress Herzen and Turgenev and Tolstoi, and if that was the case, we might think of the possibility that we are not superior to Belinskii's obsolete fatuities but may be deaf to his mighty inspiration. It is a sobering thought.

63

CHAPTER   6

PUSHKIN'S   "EVGENII ONEGIN"

BELINSKII'S longest work, his only equivalent to a full-
length book, was his series of eleven articles on Aleksandr Pushkin,
published in *Notes of the Fatherland* in 1843 and 1844. These were
an extended book review, in the grand Nineteenth Century manner, of
the first ostensibly complete edition of Pushkin's works, published
in St. Petersburg from 1838 to 1841. The edition was denounced in
the first article as slipshod and incomplete, and Belinskii hinted
clearly enough that the incompleteness was due to Nicholas's censorship as well as to editorial sloppiness. Fortunately that edition
has long since been superseded. But the articles are essentially
devoted to the works of Pushkin, to Pushkin himself – and to Russia,
humanity, the universe and all the other subjects normally covered
by Belinskii when writing for a thick journal.

It is customary in Russia to say that these articles fixed
Pushkin's place definitively as the greatest of Russian writers. In
a complicated way this is true. Pushkin had been extraordinarily
well received during his great creative burst from 1816 to 1830, but
as a marvelous contemporary rather than as a solemnly sealed
classic. From 1830 on he was under some personal clouds, and wrote
less than before, and published still less, as his earlier masterpieces faded somewhat into the past. This led to an humiliating
lessening of public esteem. When Pushkin was so viciously led into
a duel and killed in 1837, there was a tremendous wave of outrage
and sympathy, but the immediately following years did not witness
any literary revival of his works. Then came Belinskii's critique.
It was enthusiastic, but also critical at many points. It was certainly not intended to canonize Pushkin, and would not produce
that effect on any modern reader.   But according to a great deal of
testimony from contemporaries, Belinskii's work did inspire a change
of sentiment among literate Russians. Belinskii himself put his
finger on a crucial factor, the adjustment of the public over the
years to the fact that Pushkin was indeed dead and past.

"The year of the untimely death of Pushkin, as the days flow
by, recedes farther and farther from the present, and without feeling
it we get used to looking at the poetic career of Pushkin not as
interrupted but as completely finished" (1). Somehow, Belinskii's
extended, varied and, in spite of much jollity, sober reflections on
Pushkin's diverse *oeuvre* crystalized a recognition among Russians
that this was indeed a giant they had lost. Belinskii's careful

differentiation between Pushkin, the best we Russians have, and Shakespeare, a summit of all human achievement, had the effect of leading Russians to decide once and for all that Pushkin had been the Shakespeare of Russian literature. Once committed, Russians have remained loyal to Pushkin as their summit, and not even the achievement of Tolstoi has changed their judgment.

As such, Belinskii's essays on Pushkin were an extremely important moment in Russia's literary and national self-consciousness, but none of this has any effect on a modern foreign reader. Nor should we read them to find out about Pushkin and his works; Belinskii correctly assumed that his readers knew Pushkin's dramatic life and death and had read most of what he had published. We read them to find out what Belinskii thought of Pushkin, and what, therefore, was an important part of later Russian thinking about Pushkin and literature in general. We don't, of course, find modern formal criticism of Pushkin's verse techniques or language here.

There is a lot in these essays on what literature should be and on the degree to which Pushkin approximated Belinskii's ideal in his own day and in Belinskii's time. The prescriptive critic in Belinskii was out in full force. A good deal of foreign commentary on these essays has had to do with Belinskii's simultaneous championing of two contrasting literary ideals: the social purpose of literature and the autonomy of art. There are a number of glowing passages about how art is the supreme end and how the poet must be first of all a poet. There are even more vigorous passages on how literature should serve the national purpose, which readers knew to be a social-political purpose, even more in the 1840s than in Pushkin's day. Both these impulses had long co-existed in the German Romantic tradition, but the Russian political situation brought them more sharply in conflict with each other.

Both these principles had been liberal ones in Germany and were intended to be in Russia: the poet must be absolutely free *from* the authoritarian church and state, and the poet should inspire his nation to throw *off* the shackles of the authoritarian church and state. Herder and Schiller had not foreseen what began to happen in Russia in the 1840s under Belinskii: a situation in which the authoritarian church and state came to have less influence on writers and the reading public than the left *intelligentsia*, who were to dominate the journals and criticism for almost fifty years and to become a far stronger cultural and moral pressure on writers to conform to their realist modes and left convictions.

Belinskii, as we shall see, faced this dilemma by 1847. He did not yet do so in these essays on Pushkin, and so he has been charged with maintaining two inconsistent positions because he lacked the capacity to think out the deepest problems of culture. One wonders. Who *has* thought so clearly and deeply as to resolve this dilemma? Don't we all think art should be autonomous and that nothing should dictate to a poet? Don't we all think it wonderful when great literature serves a social purpose and helps mankind? Don't we all agree with Belinskii that many of the greatest writers, including both Shakespeare and Pushkin, have in many of their works achieved both, simultaneously and supremely well?

If judged by the spirit of geometry, there is an inconsistency between the two cultural ideals. But geometry may be the wrong spirit to summon up here. Notable critics, past and present, have chosen one or the other horn of the dilemma, and argued brilliantly, but we judge their arguments as *tours de force,* which slight one half of our cultural experience. Not all writers strive for or achieve formal perfection and social usefulness equally or at all. But clearly the autonomy of art *and* the usefulness of literature are both great and valid cultural values. They are difficult to embody separately and even more difficult to embody together. The feat has been achieved but past achievements provide no formula for doing it again; but it should and will be done again, in Russia and elsewhere. Is this an inconsistency or a recognition of a complex and fascinating realm?

These last paragraphs are a modern statement of a quintessentially Romantic critical position. Belinskii, living at the climax of the earlier Romantic period, did not answer the questions that bother us, but put it in the language of his time. He recognized the problem and therefore he lauded each of the two cultural values in separate paeans and in joint harmony-discord. He praised, blamed, descanted, thundered, invoked and summoned up the embodiments of both values. His language – his rhetoric we are tempted to call it – on the subject was very unlike ours, but the gist of his thought was very much like our cultivated common sense.

*   *   *

The climax of Belinskii's work on Pushkin is his treatment of the poet's *magnum opus, Evgenii Onegin.* This is a self-contained and structured piece in the eighth and ninth articles, Belinskii's most extended criticism of any one piece of literature.

"We confess", he begins, "that it is not without a certain diffidence that we enter on a critical examination of such a poem as *Evgenii Onegin ... Onegin* is Pushkin's sincerest work, the best loved child of his fantasy ... and there are few works in which the personality of the poet is shown with such fullness, brightly and clearly ... Here are his whole life, his whole soul, his whole love: here are his feelings, his understanding, his ideals ... To say nothing of the aesthetic value of *Onegin,* this poem has tremendous historical and social significance for us Russians ... Even what is weak and obsolete in *Onegin* is filled with deep significance and great interest ... Our judgment might strike many as ... contradictory, since *Onegin* is, in form, artistic to the highest degree, and in content, its demerits are its greatest value. Our entire article on *Onegin* will be a development of this idea" (2).

The article in fact develops many other ideas, but this first paragraph launches most of what follows, the central dualities if not contradictions, Belinskii's diffidence and his sovereign self-confidence, the importance of the poet's individuality and also the national collectivity, the celebrated issue of aesthetic integrity vs. social significance and the proposed paradoxical judgments which, Belinskii implies by his negative grammatical constructions, will presently be shown *not* to be contradictions.

"First of all in *Onegin* we see a poetically reproduced picture of Russian society made at one of the most interesting moments of its development" (3). The sentence would have been considerably less balanced and complex if the word "poetically" had been omitted. "*Evgenii Onegin* is an *historical* poem in the full sense of the word, although in the ranks of its heroes there is not one historical person. The historical value of this poem is all the higher because it was the first and a brilliant attempt of this kind in Russia. In this Pushkin appears not only as a poet but as the representative of a newly-awakened social consciousness" (4).

This sort of language puts modern readers off. We interpret it to mean that poetry is being dismissed as a lesser virtue, while social consciousness is valued more and history is rated highest. It is difficult for our literary world, with its contempt for history, to reconstruct imaginatively the immense domain and high human and cultural values that the Romantics referred to when they used the term, "history". To them the historical dimension enlarged and ennobled every cultural enterprise. The highest kind of painting was history painting. The grandest imaginative writing was historical or, an overlapping word, "national". Infinite was the prestige of Schiller's *Wallenstein* as would be that of Tolstoi's *War and Peace*.

Belinskii in fact used "historical" and "national" almost interchangeably in the next pages, in which he gave another version of his now familiar argument about the lack of truly Russian national poetry before Pushkin. This led to his finest blast about false nationality in literature and true: "... if you call national every play produced in which the characters are *muzhiks* [peasant men] and *babushkas*, [peasant women] bearded merchants and burgers, or in which the characters salt their artless conversation with Russian proverbs and sayings ..." (5). Belinskii obviously did not. " – according to this linden bast sandal-homespun school of thought, some stupid farce with *muzhiks* and *babushkas* is a Russian national production, but *Woe from Wit* [whose characters are all educated nobles] is Russian but not national ..." (6). On the contrary, "'True nationality', says Gogol, 'consists not of a description of a *sarafan* [a traditional Russian dress] but of the spirit of the people itself'" (7). " ... a Russian poet can show himself to be a truly national poet only by portraying in his works the life of the educated classes" (8), as Pushkin had done in *Evgenii Onegin*.

In short, Belinskii, near the beginning of Romantic nationalism in Russia, rejected the pseudo-populist foibles, misplaced emphases and vices of nationalist literature – the vices for which Western critics have blamed him for inspiring the future Communists to wallow in. He was not calling into existence Stalinist ditties about apple-cheeked peasant lasses dancing on the *kolkhoz* green, but the educated, thoughtful and profoundly national protagonists of Turgenev, Dostoevskii and Tolstoi.

Russians could not lose their nationality by becoming westernized, he insists, because national traits come from the local soil and climate. With this materialist explanation he buttresses Russia's spiritual independence! All nations 'are strings of one instrument - the spirit of humanity, but strings of differing volumes, each with its own special tone - and that is why they give out a full, harmonic chord" (9). Belinskii's nationalism did not involve any Russian version of a master-race. It was the generous, internationalist nationalism we associate with the name of his contemporary, Giuseppe Mazzini.

With these convictions Belinskii tackles the problem of how much Pushkin was imitating Byron, which has run through Russian and foreign criticism of Pushkin to our own day. "The form of a novel such as *Onegin* belongs to Byron, at least, the manner of the narrative, the mixture of prose and poetry in portraying reality, the digressions, the poet's soliloquies and especially that too perceptible intrusion of the poet's person in his own work - all that is Byron's doing" (10). These admissions and this crack at both poets would prove unacceptable to Communist critics, for whom the great Russian Pushkin could not have been imitating a vile foreigner. *But*, "Not only the contents but the spirit of Byron's poems annihilate any possibility of an essential connection between them and Pushkin's *Onegin*. Byron wrote about Europe for Europe .... Pushkin wrote about Russia for Russia ..." (11). To us this is another unparticularized assertion of the gulf between Russia and other nations. To Belinskii and his audience the statement was self-evident, important and strengthened by repetition.

Most readers of *Evgenii Onegin*, then and now, have seen Evgenii as a snobbish, cold, bored, Byronic egoist of a young nobleman, frittering his life away partly because his class had few military duties in the post-Napoleonic peace and partly because of his own self-indulgent character. During his stay at his country estate, Tatiana, a young, naive but truly fine Russian girl, falls in love with Evgenii, and declares her love in a marvelous (and now world-famous) letter. Evgenii misses the opportunity of his life by reciting to her an icy, patronizing lecture rejecting her, and leaves to waste the rest of his youth. Out of boredom and perversity, he flirts with the fiancée of his bosom friend, the Pushkin-like lyric poet Lenskii, wantonly provoking a senseless duel in which he kills the beloved songbird, and, horror-struck, flees into the interior of Russia. Years later he returns to a grand ball in St. Petersburg, whose magnificent hostess turns out to be Tatiana, now the wife of an old general and a great lady of the capital. Overcome by self-realization, a sense of lost opportunities and a sudden hopeless love, he proposes that Tatiana run off with him. She admits her undying love for him, but her family, social and moral duties require her to renounce true love and stay where fate has set her. Evgenii disappears to live unhappily forever after, a perfect tragedy and morality tale.

Belinskii, delightfully, disagreed with almost every proposition about Evgenii and Lenskii (though not about Tatiana) in the above summary of the conventional view. He leads off with an unpleasant passage near the beginning of *Evgenii Onegin*, in which

Evgenii speaks with mocking lightness of a dying uncle whom he scarcely knows, from whom he will inherit a considerable estate. Pushkin follows this up with some cynical lines on family love and the lack of it, ending with the one Herzen cited in his memoir of Belinskii, "That's what relatives are". This inspired Belinskii, as Herzen said, "to summon family life before the court and smash blood relationships to smithereens". Stuffy readers had censured Evgenii and Pushkin for this passage. Belinskii leaped to the defense of both. The kin bond, he insisted, neither does nor should automatically produce love. For Evgenii to profess love and grief for his stranger-uncle would be false and would not even be gratitude; Evgenii's benefactor is the law of entailed inheritance, Belinskii jibes, not his uncle. It would not be delicacy of human sentiment, but simply odious conventional hypocrisy, which Pushkin was placing Evgenii far above. "Pushkin acted morally in first speaking the truth, for one has to have noble courage to be the first to decide to speak the truth. And how many such truths are set forth in *Onegin*! Many of them now are neither new nor even very deep, but if Pushkin had not said them *twenty* years ago they would now be both new and deep" (12).

This paradoxical defense of Onegin is capped by another: "The greater part of the public completely denied that Onegin had a soul or a heart ..." (13). Belinskii recorded with annoyance, and he quoted forty two lines (Chapter One, stanzas 45-47) about Evgenii's disenchantment, boredom, taciturnity, dreaminess and sullen wit, which are indeed often quoted in support of such a statement. Belinskii drew the opposite conclusion from them. If Evgenii dreamed of the beauties of nature and past love affairs, then he had feeling and poetry. If he was quiet, then he felt more than he spoke. "An irascible mind is also a sign of a higher nature, because a man with an irascible mind is usually dissatisfied not only with other people but with himself" (14). Here Belinskii foreshadows Dostoevskii's psychology in *Notes from the Underground*. If Evgenii had banished all books from his study save two or three cynical modern novels, "... that speaks still more in favor of the moral superiority of Onegin, because he recognizes his portrait" (15) as few others do.

This is a fair sample of Belinskii's procedure when actually analyzing a text. He quotes an often extensive passage, and argues with it or with someone else's interpretation of it, to make a different judgment of the character portrayed or the idea set forth. It isn't really the point to track down the elusive Pushkin's actual attitudes toward Evgenii: they were surely more favorable than the public's, less favorable than Belinskii's presentation here, and more complex than both. In other works Belinskii was capable of sneering at Evgenii's selfishness. Why did Belinskii, in *this* work, *want* Evgenii to be a deep and admirable character? Not simply to praise Pushkin, who would have been well praised if credited with drawing a devastating portrait.

Over and over again (Belinskii's celebrated repetitiousness is much in evidence here), he praised Evgenii for being discontented with himself, others and society, and praised Pushkin for creating such a character. The loud, unspoken corollary was that others and society (which, unlike Evgenii, really existed) deserved discontent and contempt. Communist critics have said that the fully revolutionary Belinskii was here pointing out the half-emergent but in the end abortive revolutionary consciousness of Onegin. They jump the gun, but they are on the right track: the path from temperamental discontent and bitterness about things to conscious social-political revolt has been a broad highway in Russia. Both Pushkin and Belinskii traveled quite a way down it.

More quoted stanzas from Chapters Seven and Eight lead Belinskii to assert that "Onegin ... is not Childe Harold, not a demon, not a parody, not a fashionable fantastic, not a genius, not a great man, but simply - 'a decent chap, like you or me' [Pushkin] .... He doesn't even know what he needs, what he wants, but he knows and knows very well what he doesn't need and doesn't want, what is enough and delightful for a self-loving mediocrity. And for this, the self-loving mediocrities have not only found him 'immoral' but have denied him the passions of the heart and ardor of soul ..." (16). Things have been carried a step further. Not only is Evgenii rightly discontented, with half-emergent social consciousness, with "self-loving mediocrities" (a marvelous Aesopian euphemism, as if all that were wrong with Nicholas I's Russia was that it resembled *Main Street* and *Babbitt*), but if *you*, dear reader, think thus little of Evgenii, then you know that you are part of the unthinking reactionary counterattack!

The next stage of the argument is introduced by Belinskii's tweakingly false statement, "We have so far avoided the word *egoist*", an omnipresent word in any discussion of Evgenii, which Belinskii had quite consciously used a few pages before in preparation for a strange sermon. "Egoists come in two kinds. Egoists of the first order ... can not understand how a person can love anybody except himself .... If their affairs are going well, they are stout, fat, ruddy, jolly ..." (17). It's clear whether *these* egoists stood on the left or on the right. "Egoists of the second order ... are for the most part sick and always bored. These people often work up a passion for good deeds, for self-renunciation in the interest of others; but their problem is that they want to find happiness and pleasure in virtue, instead of aiming only at virtue in virtue" (18). How many inadequate liberals and radicals are foreshadowed here! - half the characters in Turgenev! Contrary to what we might expect, Belinskii does not place Evgenii in the second order of egoists.

"But our Onegin ... can be called an *egoist against his will* ..." (19). Belinskii quoted Chapter Two, stanzas 4 and 5, in which Evgenii abolishes *corvée* on his estate, the heavy, forced labor of the serfs, asking only for a light money-payment instead, for which the serfs blessed him but his serflord-neighbors cursed him as a nut and as a subversive. Evgenii tried to find abiding satisfaction in helping the peasants, but could not, a defect of character which Belinskii blamed not on Evgenii individually, but on the massively defective society that produced him. Belinskii could hardly condemn an egoism that produced such works.

If Belinskii was going to make ethical and social points

by rehabilitating the character of Evgenii Onegin, he knew he would have to take the bull by the horns and defend his refusal to accept Tatiana's proposal in her famous letter. His defense begins with a deliberate confusion of two genres, the novel and real life. The public is wrong to condemn Evgenii for failing to fall in love with the young Tatiana, and doubly wrong to think his later passion for the mature Tatiana proves how wrong he had been before. People often fail to fall in love with other people, Belinskii notices, no matter how abstractly suitable the matches might seem; a thousand accidents and idiosyncrasies keep the flames from lighting. "Onegin had the complete right, without any danger of being summoned before the criminal court of criticism, not to love Tatiana the girl and to love Tatiana the woman" (20). He would indeed have that right in real life, but novels are different, even realist novels. Pushkin, at the very least, was setting up the possibility that Evgenii ought to have responded to Tatiana's pure love. Belinskii, by blurring the distinction here, is among other things crying for a future truly realist tradition of novels that would annihilate the distinction, for the *Anna Karenina* that would inspire Matthew Arnold to say that it was not a work of art but a piece of life.

Switching modes, Belinskii next defends Evgenii within the novel: Evgenii, on reading Tatiana's letter, was quite properly "plunged into a sweet, pure dream" [Pushkin] , a creditable sentiment we can't object to. Switching back to a dual track within and without the novel, Belinskii justifies both Evgenii's decision to turn Tatiana down and the manner - the lecture - in which he did so. To accept her love on any terms save marriage would be inconceivably base. (Ah, the vanished past!) And marriage between a nineteen year old provincial girl and a twenty six year old metropolitan man would almost certainly not work. Her unformed character and his prematurely rigid one, her innocence and his unworthiness, her limitless potential and his passing of so many doors - Evgenii calls all these things in review in his lecture, and Belinskii chooses to join the party of readers who not only think these things are true but that Tatiana had to learn them in a painful lesson, as would be the case in real life.

Years later (actually, only two years) Evgenii, back from his Wandering Jew-like travels, meets the now mature and glorious Tatiana at the ball, and is utterly right, in Belinskii's opinion to fall completely in love with her. He "emphatically disagrees" with Pushkin's mean suggestion that Evgenii in this encounter, like all humans and our ancestor Eve, yearns for greener grass beyond the fence and forbidden fruit beyond the law. Pushkin's cynical invocation of the Christian doctrine of original sin inspires Belinskii to one of his strongest Enlightenment paeans to the goodness of human nature.

"We think better of the dignity of human nature, and are convinced that man is born not for evil but for good, not for crime but for the rational-lawful enjoyment of the good things in life, that his strivings are righteous, his instincts noble. Evil arises not from man but from society, and since society ... is still far from having reached his ideal, it is not surprising that

one sees only many crimes in him" (21). This is a very hifalutin
response to a very small, light-hearted stimulus from Pushkin, which
is also typical of Belinskii's critical procedure.

Returning to Evgenii, Belinskii approves of his letter of
love to Tatiana after the encounter at the ball. "Onegin's letter
to Tatiana burns with passion: in it there is no irony, no fashionable restraint, or fashionable mask" (22). Evgenii is now as
unhappy and sincere as any Romantic could desire. Since there is no
mention of the fact that he is now proposing adultery, we are led to
subsume that trifle under the heading of mere despicable convention.
Have we hitherto stuffily disliked Evgenii for his mocking, ironical,
self-serving detachment and lack of passion? Well, now Belinskii
tells us to admire his sudden, heedless, Romantic ardor and assault
on a basic law of God and tsar.

"What happened to Onegin afterwards? ... We don't know, and
do we need to know it when we know that the powers of this rich
nature remain without actualization, his life without meaning, and
this novel without a conclusion?" (23). This might seem to the censor to indicate that Evgenii had ruined his life, a good moralistic
point. But readers in the *intelligentsia* could be sure that
Belinskii was referring to the (sound) rumors that Pushkin had intended Evgenii to join the Decembrists in their rising against Nicholas
for constitutional liberty, a quite different moral.

This is a virtuoso performance of Belinskii's. He weaves in
and out of the novel, constantly shifting his ground, by turns divi-
ning Pushkin's hidden intent and willfully misinterpreting him,
ostensibly and actually in defense of Evgenii's character, but ultimately in defense of other actual and potential characters who feel
and are revolted by existing society, who are alienated by it,
detach themselves from it and defy it. These Onegins fall short of
fulfillment and greatness, but they so far transcend the disgusting
scene of Nicholas's Russia that no self-loving mediocrity can criticize them from this side - only gods and poets - and critics, from
beyond.

Between this great Romantic movement and the other movement
of this work, on Tatiana, is an intermezzo of opposite tonality - on
Lenskii, against Lenskii. Pushkin's original readers virtually all
loved the songbird poet and enjoyed the Romantic pangs of lamenting
his death in a duel with Evgenii in the snow. The genres of the
novel and real life became horribly confused when Pushkin was himself killed in a duel. After that, people irresistibly identified
Lenskii with Pushkin, the two murdered poets, assimilated all the
real poet's virtues to the fictional one, felt all their rage at the
real murder as they read about the one in the novel, and attributed
the whole character and fate of Lenskii to a tragic prescience of
Pushkin's own. The open-eyed Belinskii could resist this sweep of
sentiment. He didn't think much of Lenskii and was correctly certain that he had spotted many of Pushkin's sly and even mean digs at
that sort of character.

"Lenskii was a romantic both by nature and by the spirit of the
time". Belinskii used "romantic" here in his normal sense, a
person caught up in unreal sentiments and love drawn from silly

books, - an all too prominent part of Romantic culture which
Belinskii and all other aware Romantics in the larger sense despised.
"Needless to say, this was a creature devoted to everything beautiful and sublime, a pure and noble soul. But at the same time 'his
heart was gentle but ignorant:' [Pushkin]". Not a saint, but a sap!
" ... always descanting on life, he never knew it". *Knew* in the
highest Romantic sense of integrated comprehension and experience.
"Reality had no influence on him; his joys and sorrows were the
creations of his fantasy". The ultimate accolade for a poet! "He
fell in love with Olga". Belinskii thought Olga was an utterly
feather-headed drip. " ... what did it matter to him that she
didn't understand him, that on marrying him she would become a second revised edition of her mommy?" (24).

Belinskii was aware that Pushkin, although not a Lenskii-
worshipper, thought more of him than that. He distinguished, "The
poet loved the ideal embodied in Lenskii, and lamented his fall in
beautiful stanzas" (25). He quotes all three of the beautiful
stanzas (Chapter Six, stanzas 36-38), but carried the quotation
through the end of stanza 38, lines in which Pushkin, having drawn
our tears for the songbird's early death, goes on to say that
Lenskii might otherwise have lost his ardor, grown forty, fat and
flabby, and succumbed to gout. Belinskii was "convinced that the
last would undoubtedly have happened. There was much good in
him ...". Is Belinskii relenting at the end? Fear not. Read on.
" ... but the best of him was that he was young and died in time to
preserve his reputation" (26). So much for the pure lyric soul, the
Pushkin of Pushkin's own creation, for whom all literate Russia
wept!

So ends the intermezzo. Belinskii has exalted the murderer,
carefully and at some length, to a considerable height, and he has
abruptly dismissed the victim as a dundering idiot. He appears
brusquely anxious to get on with his next subject, Tatiana, but
postpones her to the next article. Intermission, with artfully
aroused expectations for the resumption of the performance next
month.

*   *   *

The ninth article on the works of Aleksandr Pushkin, the
second movement of Belinskii's tone poem on *Evgenii Onegin*, begins
with its climax and that of the whole work, an extended fortissimo
section on behalf of women which is one of the grand feminist documents of Russian and world literature. He starts with Pushkin and
Tatiana in a passage which is first connective and then assertive:
"A great merit of Pushkin is that he was the first, in his novel, to
give a poetical portrait of Russian society at that time, and in the
persons of Onegin and Lenskii he showed its dominant, i.e. masculine
side: but it is perhaps a still greater merit of our poet that he
was the first to give a poetical portrait, in the person of Tatiana,
of the Russian woman" (27).

Then he sets Pushkin and Tatiana aside for ten pages while he charges into his real subject and antagonist, Russian society. His first blow lands with a brutal suddenness that has not been surpassed, even in the 1970s: "The male, in all circumstances and in all levels of Russian society plays the leading role: we can't say that the woman has played a secondary, inferior role, because she hasn't played any role at all" (28). The devotee of George Sand knew the low position of women in Europe, and was the more outraged by the depths below depths of women's position in Russia. He wasn't having any of the notion that male Russians were now Europeanized and therefore treated women decently. "Nowadays even our *respected* merchantry with a beard from which is wafted a *leetle* smell of cabbage and onion walks down the street with the *better half* arm in arm instead of shoving her with his knee from behind, showing the way and ordering her to look to one side; but at home - why speak of what happens at home? Why bring one's filth out of the house?" (29).

The outraged protest against men's reduction of women to the domestic sphere, and against women's collaboration in this had long been a frequent, great and noble Romantic theme, and from this inspiration the organized women's movements of the civilized world would soon arise. Belinskii, in the first year of his problematic marriage, was ringing the changes with wicked abandon - no qualifications or subtleties in *these* passages:

"Why is it that here we don't understand and don't want to understand what woman is, don't feel any need for her, don't want her and don't seek her, in a word, here there aren't any women. For us, the "fair sex" exists only in novels, tales, plays and elegies; but in reality it is divided into four categories: little girls, marriageable women, married women and finally old maids and old women. The first, just children, nobody is interested in; the last everybody fears and hates (and often with cause); consequently our fair sex consists of two divisions: of girls who ought to be married and of women who are already married. A Russian girl is not a woman in the European sense of the word, not a human being: she is nothing else than a *bride* .... Still in the cradle she is told by mother, father, sisters, brothers, nannies, nurses and everybody around her that she will be a bride and has to have suitors. Hardly has she reached her twelfth year than mother says to her, 'Aren't you ashamed of yourself, miss, you're almost a *bride*!'. No wonder that after that she ... can't look at herself as ... a human being but sees herself only as a *bride*. No wonder that from her earliest years to late adolescence, sometimes even to the depths of old age, all her thoughts, all dreams, all efforts, all prayers are concentrated on one *idée fixe*: on marriage - that getting married is her only passionate desire, the purpose and idea of her existence, that except for this she understands nothing, thinks of nothing, wants nothing .... Is she to blame for this? From her eighteenth year she already begins to feel that she is not the daughter of her parents, not the beloved child of their hearts ... but a tiresome burden, goods threatening to become stale, unneeded furniture which at any moment may fall in price and can't be gotten rid of" (30). Belinskii can generate metaphors of human beings transformed into market commodities as well as Dickens in capitalist England.

"... and what does an anxious mama teach her daughter? – to flirt with calculation, to pretend to be an angel, to hide, under the soft, smooth fur of a kitten's paws, the claws of a cat. And whatever the poor daughter's own nature might be, she involuntarily enters into the role which has been given her in life" (31).

Nor do we imagine, by this time, that Belinskii will be delighted with the life of the Russian married woman. "And the recent bride, now the young wife? – Oh, she has her 'heart's content!'. She has finally reached the goal of her life .... She can have her caprices and fall into faints, she can madden her husband, children and servants. She doesn't lack for anything: carriage – no carriage, shawl – no shawl, all the expensive toys she wants ... The content of conversations is scandal and dress, dress and scandal. God has blessed this marriage every year with a child. How is she going to bring up her children? The same way she was brought up by her mommy ... nurses and mammies ... will explain them the differences between house-goblins and wood-goblins, witches and water-witches ... And now they grow up: the father does what he wants with the boys, while the girls learn ... to lace themselves up ... to plink on the pianoforte, to gabble in French ... and after that their one study, their one occupation is to ensnare suitors ..." (32).

Stop. Pause. Change of direction and tone, and then the climatic paragraph: "And would you blame her for all this? What gives you the right to demand of her that she be different from what you yourself have made her? Can you blame even her parents? Haven't you yourself made of woman only a bride and a wife and nothing more? Have you ever approached her disinterestedly, simply, without any designs .... Have you ever wanted to have a friend in a woman you were not in love with, a sister in a woman who was not related? – No! .... If you ever pay serious attention to a woman it is for the determined purpose of marriage or lechery. Your view of women is purely utilitarian, almost commercial: for you she is capital with interest, an estate to marry, a home with profit; if not this, then a cook, laundress, housekeeper, nurse; a big deal if she's an odalisque" (33).

This is one of the grandest rages of Raging Vissarion. Its effectiveness comes from the justice of its cause and from the interlacing of vehement and ludicrous words and phrases – and not a little from its multiple targets. If the dominant roar is at the patriarchal establishment, there is also plenty of ferocious hatred of upper class women as such, and is it going too far to think, women as such? – and a few clawings at household serfs in their ignorance. The drive against injustice is fueled by a magnificent spleen. So it was to be with many later feminist writers, men and women alike. Every Russian in the woman's cause read this tirade and was inspired by it. It is clearly the pattern in argument, method and emotion of Tolstoi's more extended and detailed but scarcely more Olympian rages in the culminating work of Russian feminist literature, *The Kreutzer Sonata*.

The reader wonders how Belinskii will climb down from his peak of Prophetic denunciation and pessimism to deal with Tatiana. He changes his tone and subject, but without leaving his venom and gloom: "But amid this world of morally twisted phenomena, there are occasionally truly colossal exceptions, which always pay dearly for their uniqueness and become victims of their own superiority. Natures of genius, not recognizing their genius, they are mercilessly killed by an unconscious society as a propitiatory sacrifice for its sins. - Such was Pushkin's Tatiana" (34).

But Belinskii presently cheers up and makes fun of Tatiana's family, as Pushkin did, even quoting her father's pseudopious and rank-proud epitaph, "An humble sinner, Dmitri Larin/God's servant and a brigadier" (35). Tatiana is so much more than her family can account for that Belinskii invokes Russia, rather than her family to explain her. "The nature of Tatiana is not complicated but it is deep and strong. In Tatiana there were none of those morbid contradictions which afflict excessively complex characters: Tatiana is cut from one whole cloth .... Her whole life is imbued with that integrity, that unity, which in the world of art constitutes the supreme merit of a work of art" (36).

The overcomplex characters in European and Russian Romantic literature before and after Belinskii, were almost entirely male. Belinskii stood with many critics and most of society here in thinking women were God's saving healthy unity, deep and strong, the waters of Shiloh and the Rock of Gibraltar. This classic judgment in favor of women's nature melts into a Classical judgment in favor of noble simplicity in works of art. These values were not often parts of Romantic psychological and artistic practise, but were frequently, as here, one part of Romantic ideals.

"Tatiana is a rare and beautiful flower ..." (37) an age-old male metaphor for women. Belinskii quotes Pushkin's lines to describe her situation, "Unknown in the dense grass/To butterfly or bee". Pushkin had composed these lines to describe her sister Olga, but Belinskii corrects the poet with sovereign critical highhandedness by saying "These two lines ... apply much more to Tatiana" (38). She reads deep French books *and* shares Russian peasant superstitions, an admirable fusion of both worlds. She has many negative virtues: she is not ambitious; she is not a Laodicean, "lukewarm natures that are neither cold nor hot" (39), whom Belinskii would certainly have spewed out of his mouth. Belinskii may have been the first Russian secular moralist to use this famous passage from Revelations repeatedly to praise a Romantic vehemence of character and idealism. He was followed by many of the *intelligentsia*, not just by Dostoevskii.

His Russian and Romantic dislike of moderation continues: "Tatiana is an exceptional being, a deep, loving and passionate nature. Love, for her, would be either the greatest blessing or the greatest misfortune of her life, without any mediating middle. With the joy of reciprocal love such a woman is a steady, bright flame; in the contrary case ... it is the more destructive and touching for being enclosed within" (40). This passage expresses a traditional male rather than a feminist concept of a good woman. Tolstoi would quote it thirty years later when working on *Anna Karenina*, a woman whom he set up in the position of Tatiana at the end of *Evgenii Onegin*, and had make the other choice.

When Belinskii comes to Tatiana's famous letter proposing to
Evgenii, he can really do no more than quote at length and worship
it: "... a supreme expression of a revealed woman's heart ..." (41)
although he admits that it seems more "romantic" (in the narrow
sense) as the years go by.

But Belinskii has a great deal to say about Tatiana's last
encounter with Evgenii in Chapter Eight. Tatiana has become a great
lady of the capital, moving easily and triumphantly in its
Europeanized world. She accuses herself of having degenerated
thereby since the days when she was a naive, provincial Russian girl.
Pushkin presumably wanted us to think she was both right and wrong
but wonderful to feel thus stricken, but Belinskii's ideology forced
him to reject the complexity. His view of Russia was that it *should*
become westernized and therefore more civilized but no less Russian:
so his view of Tatiana, who embodied more than Russian womanhood for
him, had to be that *her* westernization and sophistication had done
her only good, proved all the more by her noble Russian inability to
be proud of it. She was greater, more tragic and more supremely
Russian than ever.

Belinskii had praised Evgenii in the first article for
passionately proposing adulterous love. Here he involves himself in
a paradox by praising Tatiana for refusing him. He quotes, with
exclamations of admiration, the last two lines of her speech to
Evgenii, "But I was given to another/I shall be true to him forever"
(42). "'But I *was given* to another' ... not '*I gave myself*'!
Eternal faithfulness - *to whom* and in *what*? Faithfulness in relations which are a profanation of feeling and of feminine chastity,
for some relations, unsanctified by love, are to the highest degree
immoral ..." (43). Is this a condemnation of Tatiana? It is a
treacherous and subversive passage. He mocks the traditional ethic,
that sexual relations unsanctified by God and the law are to the
highest degree immoral, by substituting the central Romantic claim,
"unsanctified by love", which condemns most of society's marriages
while approving of loving adultery. We may assume that Belinskii had
long since condemned society utterly; it is Tatiana whom these sentences seem to condemn, for assenting to and justifying to Evgenii
the vile social order and its obscene values..

But the turn is coming. All Russian readers knew that
Pushkin was on Tatiana's side here. Belinskii had a paradox to climb
out of. "The life of a woman is strongly centred in the life of her
heart. For her to live means to love and to love means to sacrifice.
For this role nature made Tatiana, but society remade her" (44).
Unusually crushing Russian society remade her, not just oppressed
her but genuinely remade her; she genuinely internalized some of its
values, as Russian women must. Belinskii says she is not Vera in
Lermontov's *Hero of Our Time*, who does betray marriage for love.
"Vera is more the woman, but thereby more the exception, while
Tatiana is the type of the Russian woman. Enthusiastic idealists ...
demand that ordinary women scorn the opinion of society. That is a
lie; a woman cannot scorn the opinion of society; but she may sacrifice it modestly, without phrases and without self-praise, if she
understands the full magnitude of her sacrifice, the full weight of
the contempt she brings on herself in obeying another, higher law,

the law of her nature, and her nature is love and self-sacrifice" (45)

Belinskii has complicatedly climbed out of his paradox into a quite different one: Society and its arranged, loveless marriages are unspeakable and the male Evgenii was right to propose revolt against them for true love. But women are different. It is terribly wrong to oppress them but they are inspiringly right to endure and to sacrifice themselves continuingly even for the sake of society's wrong dictates. Ordinary -European - women may leave marriage for true love if they acquiesce in society's wrongful retribution. But Russian women are even more crushed by society than European women, so their resultant nature is even more shining. A really Russian woman such as Tatiana will not even acquiesce in society's wrongful retribution for the sake of true love. She will make the greater, the truly Russian self-sacrifice of renouncing even her true love to maintain the values in which society has wrongly crushed her into believing.

This is not a radical and/or Romantic position of Belinskii's. It is not a conservative and/or Christian position either. It was not Pushkin's view. It is indeed a paradoxical position and a tragic one. It was a foreshadowing and almost certainly a source of many things in the future Russian novel.

Our responses to this are a paradox, too. Belinskii's grand feminist tirade at the beginning of the second article seemed inspiringly egalitarian and heartwarmingly modern, but the rest of the article turns out to be neither. Belinskii did not here think that women are equal to men; he thought they are superior, but in ways which modern women and men cannot accept. Male oppression has made women more self-sacrificing and therefore better than men. His widely shared conviction was the brother of the Russian Romantic-nationalist conviction that Russians are nobler than other peoples because of their age-old oppressions, and the child of the Christian belief that the humble downtrodden will be saved before the high and mighty. Many people today hold a similar view of blacks and whites.

Most feminists in the last 200 years, men and women alike, have believed that women are in some sense superior to men, but the content of the earlier feminist conviction, exemplified here by Belinskii, is revolting to the present generation. Our Romantic feminist predecessors, including Belinskii, while aware of infinite individual variations, were deeply convinced that women are essentially simple and men essentially complex, that women are emotional and men intellectual, that men are driving and ambitious while women are passive and loving, that men are sexual while women are nurturing, that men are oppressive and debased while women are oppressed and purified, that men are rebellious and easily discouraged while women are accepting and enduring unto death and beyond, and that all this is exactly what is so nobly superior in women.

To us this is nauseating, for men and women alike have now lost the faith that self-abnegation is the highest trait of character. But in the Nineteenth Century this was the prevailing view of most of the greatest psychological and moral documents of the age, which we ourselves call *realist* novels. And famously, there was no tradition of the realist novel more centred on this view of men and women than the one which Belinskii, in this and other works, is credited with having called forth, the Russian realist novel.

Having used *Evgenii Onegin* to launch into this Romantic-nationalist-feminist sermon, which by its position in the structure of his essay and by its verbal power is its climax and main point, Belinskii, in a kind of code, rephrases his praise and concludes with a long quotation. "*Onegin* could be called an encyclopaedia of Russian life and to the highest degree a national work .... It was an act of consciousness for Russian society, almost the first .... That step was a *bogatyr*'s [an heroic warrior of the Russian ballads] stride, and after it there was no longer any possibility of standing in one place ..." (46).

A work of literature broke Russia's icy bonds and began to push the nation forward! No one, no tsar, could now stop the process, but other writers can push Russia still farther forward. It was in this Belinskiian context that Herzen said, "a great writer is a kind of second government of his country".

CHAPTER 7

"A VIEW OF RUSSIAN LITERATURE IN 1846"

BELINSKII'S last job was as dynamo-in-residence at the thick journal, the *Contemporary*. The journal had been founded by Pushkin,
had died, had suffered several attempts at resurrection, and was
refounded with new capital and new talent late in 1846. Its big
coup was the capture of Belinskii from *Notes of the Fatherland*, at
which he had been working since it first lured him to St. Petersburg
in 1839. The *contemporary* offered him 2,000 rubles for the year
1847, the largest salary he ever made, which he certainly needed,
for he was now a family man with a wife and daughter, and a new
baby expected in the new year. But he said he would never have
moved if he had not been offered a free hand, by which he meant
freedom to write and publish what he thought best, limited by the
censorship, of course, but not by other editors, - and if he had
not been attracted by the group of editors and writers.

Of these the chief was another of Belinskii's discoveries,
the young poet Nikolai Nekrasov (1821-1878), who was rescued almost
from starvation by this new venture. He would become editor-in-
chief in 1848, steer the journal through Nicholas I's Seven Mad
Years of frenzied police terror (1848-1855) and preside over its
flowering in the later 1850s and 1860s as the major organ of the
new radical generation, the vehicle of Chernyshevskii and
Dobroliubov. And he would be the major poet of what Belinskii predicted would be a thin age of Russian poetry, the popular, radical
poet of the hardships of peasant life and of their stoic endurance,
poems such as *Red Nosed Frost* and *Who Can Be Happy in Russia*?
which are intensely admired by the Communists. Belinskii was only
able to help Nekrasov for a year and a half, quite sufficient to
give the refounded journal a tremendous start. His position at the
Contemporary was the post at which Belinskii died.

One of the projects on which Belinskii set the highest
importance was a projected annual review of Russian literature, to
appear in the first number of each new year. And indeed he did
write *A View of Russian Literature in 1846*, which appeared in the
first issue of the refounded *Contemporary* in January, 1847. (The
Russian word translated as "view" is *"vzgliad"*, which like many
Russian words is vague in the time it refers to; it can mean anything from a rapid "glance" to a lengthy "survey").

As anyone who has attempted anything of the sort knows, a

review of the books published in any one year is a splendid idea but an impossible one to organize and work out. Probably in response to this problem, rather than on any theoretical grounds, Belinskii planned his work so as to devote about 60% of it to general reflections on subjects from the Slavophiles to the nature of nationality and only about 40% to books of poetry and novels actually published in 1846.

Belinskii begins by granting himself complete license to discuss everything: "The present is the result of the past and an indication of the future. Therefore to talk about Russian literature in the year 1846 means talking about the contemporary condition of Russian literature in general, which can't be done without considering what it was and what it must be" (1). When we think that by "literature" Belinskii meant not just *belles-lettres* but everything published, we realize how wide a franchise he was giving himself. Of course readers who have reached this point know that Belinskii usually managed to include his views on what Russian literature had been and should be no matter what subject he was supposed to be writing on.

"The main purpose of our article is to make known to the reader of the *Contemporary* beforehand its view on Russian literature and consequently its spirit and direction as a journal" (2). This asserts, directly, the centrality of literature in thought and serious life. Equally striking, when one thinks of it, is Belinskii's assertion of his own primacy in the journal. This was an unsigned article and it allegedly spoke for the combined publishers and editors, but here was Belinskii insisting that *this* article, clearly recognizable as his by its marked idiosyncrasies of style and opinion, was the determining one.

"This article, together with the article by the editor himself ... will be a second, *inner* prospectus of the *Contemporary*, by which the readers themselves can verify whether our promises have been kept" (3). This was a noble, anti-commercial protestation. It also granted someone else a share in the journal, for Belinskii did not write the editorial – but at the same time one can detect a monitory riding herd on his colleagues to keep them up to the mark, Belinskii's mark.

In the long second paragraph he begins a recapitulation of his by now well known views on Russian literature, which he had published at length in at least a dozen articles since *Literary Reveries* in 1834. The next ten pages would be his last such survey, much of which is now familiar to us (Lomonosov once again begins Russian literature in 1739 by sending in from Germany his *Ode on the Taking of Khotin*), but some of it is new. It contains at once his strongest attack on and defense of Lomonosov, who gave to the Russian literature he was founding "a bookish, imitative direction", who was "this rhetorician in poetry" (4).

The defense is threefold. First, an argument by one of the biological metaphors of the Nineteenth Century: "Foreign content taken from outside can never compensate either in literature or in life for the absence of one's own national content; but it may be transformed into it in time, as the food a man takes from outside is transformed into blood and muscle, and sustains strength, health and life in him" (5). Second, a defense from the common Nineteenth Century argument, now called Marxist after a late one of the many thinkers who shared it, that culture is a function of the societal base. This was really an elaboration of his earlier theses that Peter's Russia was new and raw, so it could only give birth to Lomonosov's immensely important but modest poetic talent.

And finally, a considerable defense against the charge of rhetoric itself, earlier so freely made. Lomonosov wrote both scientific works and *belles-lettres*. In his writings on astronomy, physics, chemistry, metallurgy and navigation Belinskii finds no rhetoric (though they were written in long Latin-German periods with all the verbs at the end). His substantive writing reflected his direct knowledge of and work in these scientific materials. But there was no material for his poetry in the then primitive public life of his country, so he had to borrow material from foreign cultures, not at home on Russian soil, and therefore rhetorical in expression. To us this is casuistry; his contemporaries might recognize the Hegelian source of these ideas about the dependence of art on society and the influence of one culture on another.

What if Lomonosov, instead of importing French Neoclassicism, had invented in Russia, three generations ahead of its time, a German model, folkish, nationalist Romanticism? "The question is perfectly silly, like questions such as, what if Peter the Great had been born in France and Napoleon in Russia, or what if winter, instead of being followed by spring, were succeeded immediately by summer?" (6). Belinskii was always impatient with efforts to base the nation on its folk culture.

This round of Belinskii's discussions of the Age of Karamzin displayed a radicalization of Hegel's ideas of the evolutionary stages of society and culture. Do people complain that Karamzin's literary influence is "backward" and "damaging" now (in the 1840s)? It is for it survives way beyond its day, the past weighing down the present and the future. But his literary influence could not have lasted so far beyond its day as to become oppressive if it had not been new, vital, beautiful and great in its own appropriate time. Two pages later, Belinskii states innocently that, "Outside the world of *belles lettres* itself, the influence of Karamzin is still very considerable" (7). This would be his political influence on the far right, and Belinskii could count on his readers remembering – for two pages – his Left Hegelian argument about influences being backward and damaging when they lasted way beyond the period in which they arose.

Now Belinskii transposes through several chords to his next movement and theme: "This is best shown in the so-called *slavophile* party. It is well known that in the eyes of Karamzin Ivan III was higher than Peter the Great, and the pre-Petrine *Rus'* better than the new Russia. This was the source of the so-called slavophiles, whom we reckon ... to be a very important development, proving that the ripe and mature period of our literature is near" (8). A most left-handed compliment!

This opens Belinskii's ten page discussion of the Slavophiles, perhaps the most important section of *A View of Russian Literature in 1846*. The Slavophiles were several loose circles of Russian thinkers, writers, composers and artists from the 1830s through the 1870s, a professedly nativist Russian response to the European cultural onslaught of the preceding 150 years, though they themselves were much inspired by conservative German Romantic thinkers such as Schelling, and some were supremely adept at preaching Russianism in such European forms as the journal, the novel and the opera.

Prominent among Slavophile convictions were a vigorously reasserted Orthodox Christianity as opposed to Western secularism, a full-fledged Russian nationalism on the Romantic model, a consequent idealization of the peasant Russian people in their faith and their rich folk culture, a yearning for Kievan and Muscovite *Rus'* before Peter the Great, when it was allegedly purely Russian and Christian, a disesteem for all the supposed Western progress of the St. Petersburg era, a profound belief that the apparently primitive characteristics of Russians - deep faith, humility, irrationality, communal solidarity, technological backwardness and indifference to time, money and competition - were greatly morally superior to modern, secular, industrial Europe, and for many Slavophiles, a belief that Russia was the Messiah nation whose spiritual fire would survive the storm and revive the Europe that would soon destroy itself. Clearly Belinskii disagreed with the Slavophiles totally on every one of these points. He had lived with them and enjoyed battling with them in conversation and in print for more than twelve years. But in this article his approach is interestingly different.

Belinskii now drops the deprecating "so-called"s and say straightforwardly, "First of all slavophilism is a conviction, which, like all convictions, deserves our full respect, even if, as in this case, we completely disagree with it" (9). This sounds strange if we do not continually keep in mind the numerous and prominent self-serving hypocrites lacking any sincere conviction, always produced by tyrannies such as Nicholas's. Belinskii demanded that one blow either cold or hot, and the Slavophiles at least blew cold, for which they too were in continual trouble with the régime. "We have many slavophiles and their number is always growing, a fact which also speaks in favor of slavophilism" (10). This also seems strange to us but less so to one who still believed that in some senses the real is the rational and the rational is the real. "One could say that the whole of our literature and part of the public ... is divided into two schools, the slavophiles and the non-slavophiles" (11). "Non-Slavophile" was a safe way of mentioning the dissident portion of the *intelligentsia* that called themselves Westerners.

"Much could be said in favor of slavophilism in speaking of the causes which produced this phenomenon; but on closer examination it is impossible not to see that the existence and importance of this literary coterie is purely negative, that it has been called into existence and lives not for its own sake but in order to justify and promote the very idea it set itself to struggle against" (12). The desire to fend off the censorship must have helped make this sentence so abstract and tangle-footed, for there was a lot of forbidden Hegelianism in it: Belinskii thought of the Slavophiles as a purely nativist opposition to westernizing Russia, as

reactionaries in the original sense of the term. But the *function* he thought the Slavophiles were serving in the history of Russia was to criticize, and needle, and thereby to refine and aid the Westerners' drive to transform Russia. For this purpose the Slavophiles had been "called into existence", not consciously by themselves, certainly not by any Orthodox God, but by a Left Hegelian version of the ineluctable logic of history.

"Therefore it's of no interest to talk to the slavophiles about what they want .... The fact is that the positive side of their doctrine amounts to some kind of foggy, mystical presentiment of the victory of the East over the West, the unlikelihood of which is all too clearly demonstrated by the facts of reality ..." (13). This, in spite of its abstractions, was a model for all future unsympathetic left and later Communist rejections of the Slavophiles, down to the core assertion that what is mystical must be foggy. It also played close to the censor's wrath, for while Nicholas's régime was very far from the Slavophiles' idea of Christian Russia, it was actively hostile to any such prediction of an inevitable victory of the West over the East.

Then comes the heart of Belinskii's views of the Slavophiles, and his tribute to them: "The negative side of their teaching deserves much more attention, not for their criticisms of the supposedly decaying West (the slavophiles are completely unable to understand the West because they measure it with an eastern rod) but for their criticisms of Russian Europeanism, about which they say a lot that is sound, which one can't help half-agreeing with, for example, that there is a kind of duality in Russian life, consequently a lack of moral unity; that this deprives us of a definite national character such as distinguishes, to their credit, almost all the European nations; that this makes us into a kind of caught-in-between mind, which can think well in French, German and English but which can't think in Russian; and that the cause of all this is the reform of Peter the Great. This is all correct ..." (14).

Belinskii, in this important passage, was crediting the Slavophiles with the discovery and first philosophical examination of the since famous phenomenon of the dual society, of Russian cultural schizophrenia, of the tearing apart of the individual souls of the Russian *intelligentsia* and of the whole country's cultural life by a westernization that had gone too far to be rolled back but not far enough to have transformed the nation yet – the model of the cultural split that was to be repeated in hundreds of semi-westernized societies around the world. Belinskii mentions here the intellectual disorientation brought on by this split, but he intimates recognition of the attendant psychic agony, of the famous "sick, split, Russian soul", which, as he knew, was central to the Slavophiles' concept. In recognizing here that the Slavophiles had made a genuine and important discovery, Belinskii legitimized all future left recognition and study of the phenomenon. If Belinskii admitted the problem, then it was not betraying the progressive cause of the Westerners to do so.

"We must not stop with the recognition of the correctness of a fact, but should examine the causes of it in hopes of finding in

the evil itself a way out of it" (15). This was one of the many
Romantic statements of the thought now most famous in Marx's version
of it, "Philosophers have hitherto tried to understand the world;
the point, however, is to change it". Belinskii went on, "This the
slavophiles have not done and have not tried to do, but this is what
they have led their opponents if not to achieve then to try. And
this is their true service. To fall asleep in self-admiring dreams,
whether of national glory or of our Europeanism, is equally fruit-
less and harmful ... and we must say thank you to those who wake us
from such a sleep" (16). Belinskii's convoluted prose here let him
get past the censor his statement that Nicholas's propagandists had
fallen asleep in self-admiring dreams of national glory. But his
main point was that the Slavophiles had really hit a raw nerve, had
really stung awake the too complacent Westerners when they needed it,
to begin the effort to deal with Russia's cultural schizophrenia.
No Slavophile would be flattered by this praise of Belinskii's, but
his unwonted modesty – even Belinskii does not claim to know the
cure yet for the psychological and social tensions of a dual society,
only that people must start to examine the problem – and the whole
tone of the passage indicate that his tribute to the Slavophiles
here was not ironical or left-handed but quite sincere.

But even after such a rare admission of trouble within the
progressive ranks, Belinskii's optimism rises again indomitably.
The Slavophiles are not right in saying that the reforms of Peter
the Great deprived Russian of nationality; the core of Belinskii's
ideology denied that. No, Peter's Europeanizing work has been concluded successfully, and now it is time for the next stage.

"It is time for us to stop *becoming* and to begin to *be* ....
It is time for us to stop admiring the European simply because it is
not Asiatic, but to love, respect and strive for it simply because
it is *human*, rejecting everything European that is not human ...
with the same energy that we reject everything Asiatic that is not
human" (17). Belinskii would surely have been grateful for the as
yet future metaphor of "growing pains", to describe this cultural
split. He uses his familiar metaphors of growth and maturity to
characterize the split and its hoped-for healing. The mere metaphors do not persuade us, but Belinskii's intense hope that the
schism would be ended has been felt around the world ever since.
Can India be a modern democracy and preserve its cultural heritage?
Is there a Peruvian solution to economic development? What is
Canadian art?

The Slavophiles "... admitting the necessity for a higher
national principle, and not finding one in the real world ...
vaguely suggest to us that *humility* is the characteristic of Russian
nationality" (18). This now world-famous Slavophile thesis, then in
its infancy, so irritated Belinskii that he devoted the last three
pages of his discussion of Slavophilism to rebutting it.

"Humility is, in certain circumstances, a very praiseworthy
virtue in a man of any country ..." (19). That "in certain circumstances" is deadly. But Russians and Russian history have not been
noted for humility, and he is obviously glad of it. He runs through
the history of early Russia, delighting that its princes were more

distinguished for arrogance and truculence than humility. He gleefully cites treacherous rulers who were crafty, not meek. Then there were the two Ivans called "Groznii" - the Dread or the Terrible - not the Humble. "They talk of *love*, too, as a national principle found only in the Slavonic tribes ..." (20). Belinskii can't stand that one either, and lists with adolescent relish the many assassinations, the prevailing tortures, the general horror of Russian history.

Why this revulsion against humility and love, this delight in proving that Russia had little of them? Some of it was a progressive desire to cancel the conservatives' praise of the past as a weapon in the current political battle. But much of it was clearly a dislike of the personal qualities of humility and love as defined by the Slavophiles, who, like many other Christians and many in other religions, valued humility in the sense of voluntarily abnegating one's own active intelligence, will, assertiveness and efforts to control the fate of others and oneself, and valued love in the sense of non-discriminatory benevolent feelings toward others, whether they were one's family or one's torturers. The effort to control events was surrendered to God, who Himself, when on earth, lived an humble, loving, passive, meek, surrendering life (far more so in the eyes of the Orthodox than of Western Christians).

Belinskii was speaking not only for secularists and radicals, but for all self-consciously assertive and autonomous people - Lenin, Rockefeller and Nietzsche alike - in rejecting all this, not only because he thought humility was being hypocritically preached by the churches to keep peasants and other enslaved groups from even wanting to break their chains, but also because he thought these were revolting traits of any developed human personality, anti-intellectual, cowardly, weak, namby-pamby and disgusting. To be thus humble and loving, Belinskii believed, was to surrender control not to benevolent Providence but to serflords and to Nicholas. He would have been glad to say with Sartre, a century later, "I despise those who love their executioners".

It is interesting that Belinskii, unlike most men who have felt this way (including Nietzsche, Rockefeller and Lenin), systematically refused to add "womanish" to his series of negative adjectives describing the humble. And we remember how Belinskii had praised Tatiana and the women of Russia whom she typified to the skies (if not to Heaven) exactly for their renunciation of personal fulfillment and submission to injustice - though he never used the word "humility" in that discussion. Inconsistency? Uncleansed male chauvinism? Romantic acceptance of the contrary tendencies of life? We are often like Belinskii in this: we are mostly secularists who train ourselves to be masters of our fate, but most of us are deeply moved by the works of the greatest of the Slavophiles, Dostoevskii, the most powerfully and disturbingly alien and yet innerly relevant glorifications of humility that we know.

Belinskii's review of the history of Russian literature led him to the Slavophiles and their ideas about Russia which he found of such unequal worth. Now, sufficiently warmed up by smiting the false, vile side of their ideas, he launches into one of his great tone poems - or grand tirades - on his favorite subject, which must seem obsessive by this time, man and nation. Its structure is a grand metaphorical proportion: personality is to a man as nationality is to humanity, and this is worked out as intricately and extendedly as any Seventeenth Century English Metaphysical poet could have done it.

It all begins with an apparent traditional presentation of body and soul. Our souls, we have been taught, are noble and eternal, while our bodies are low and corruptible. Belinskii will certainly not leave us with what Russian children were taught. Perhaps we despise our bodies because we know so little about them. Doctors, he says, know much more and respect the body much more.

He advances another metaphorical relation: the agronomist who respects not only the rich harvest of grain but the earth itself which has produced it, and even the manure which increases the earth's fertility. The manure remains in the earth for the censor, but will float into our idea of the human body, the preceding metaphor, which is now resumed. We value our feelings, then shouldn't we value the lump of flesh called the heart, which beats fast or slow in faithful response to every movement of our soul? The science here is not actually false, but it is being used to invoke the traditional false identification of the heart as the seat of the emotions.

We foresee the next metaphor: we highly respect the human mind? Then let us marvel at unfathomable intricacies of the physical human brain, without which there is no mind. "Psychology which is not based on physiology has no substance .... Mind without body ... is a dream of logic, a lifeless abstraction" (21). So much, dear censor, for God! "Mind is man in the flesh, or, a better way of saying it, man through the flesh, in a word, *personality*" (22). Theology is being blasphemously parodied to assert Nineteenth Century materialism. If you are in love with a woman, it isn't the moral qualities of her mind and heart that you love; if it were, you would drop her when a more moral woman appeared "as a good book is dropped for a better one" (23). Our Twentieth Century theology of sex is being blasphemously parodied in advance to assert Nineteenth Century materialism.

There follows a paragraph of lyric praise for the infinite variety and excellence of human personality, no variety of which would be possible without the intricate and equally excellent body common to all. This is very Aristotelian without explicit intent: what Belinskii calls "personality" (*lichnost'*) is any one of the innumerable *forms* of the basic *matter*, which he calls "man".

Yet this is only half of the proportion, of the tone poem. Belinskii now states the full proportion: "What *personality* is in relation to the *idea* of man, *nationality* is in relation to the *idea* of humanity" (24). Russian schoolchildren would be able to cancel out "idea" which appears on both sides of the proportion. "In other words, nationality is the personality of humanity. Without nationality, humanity would be a lifeless logical abstraction .... On this question I am ready to side with the slavophiles ..." (25). Belinskii vigorously reasserts his agreement with the great majority of Romantic Europe: nationality (certainly not class) is

the primary category into which humanity is divided. But this side
of the metaphorical proportion makes not one point but two: our
humanity is as common as our nationalities are separate. A nation,
so conceived, should neither dominate other nations nor withdraw
into Chinese isolation, should not engage in rivalries, wars or even
invidious comparisons. This is another grand expression of
Belinskii's broad, generous egalitarian nationalism, Mazzini's, not
Hitler's.

Belinskii then writes wishfully, "In our time national
rivalries and antipathies have entirely died out. A Frenchman no
longer hates an Englishman simply because he is an Englishman, and
the other way round" (26). A year later the equally unprophetic
Marx and Engels were to write, "The workingman has no country ....
National differences and antagonisms are vanishing gradually from
day to day". This was a widespread conviction of the European left
Romantics as the Napoleonic Wars receded decades into the past.

But Belinskii would put this supposed phenomenon to use in
quite a different way from Marx. If it were the case, then Russian
reactionaries were wrong and Russian liberals were right: Russians
could fearlessly borrow the best from Europe without ceasing to be
Russian. And once again he predicted and called for the adult
period of Russian literature, which he barely lived into the beginning of, when Russians took the Western novel, painting and opera
and in these foreign forms created the maturest masterpieces of
Russian culture.

At the very end of his tone poem, genius is brought into the
discussion in yet another proportion. What is potential in a
nation is realized in a genius - Aristotle through Hegel. "A
nation has the same relation to its great men as the soil to the
plants which it brings forth" (27). A great poet must be supremely
national, for otherwise he can't be great. - This was one of
Belinskii's grandest poems in expression of his most important and
most intensely held ideas.

*   *   *

Here we are, three fifths of the way through a fifty page
essay which, we may have forgotten, was called *A View of Russian
Literature in 1846*. He has discussed all of Russian literature and
the world, as he had promised, and now he fulfills the lesser part
of his promise and writes about what was actually published in
Russia in 1846.

Russia was still behind Europe, he thought, and was still
working at literary problems which Europeans had solved long ago.
Readers heard the unspoken parallel about politics here. Conversely,
Europeans were working out problems which Russians should not tackle
yet. He stands Terence on his head: "We can and should be interested in them, for nothing human should be alien to us if we want to

be human ... but we should play the role of Don Quixotes if we got excited about them" (28). If the Communists are right that Belinskii was referring not to the European literary avant-garde but to socialism here, then his attitude toward it was rather distant.

He advances as evidence of the maturity of Russian literature the diminution of poetry. A generation back, versifiers sprang up everywhere, and "grew like mushrooms after a rain" (29), - a particularly Russian simile. "Not so now. Verse play a subordinate role compared to prose" (30). These sentences don't deprecate poetry, which Belinskii had shown he loved with a passion. They express his conviction, paralleled by some other radical critics in Europe, that the social period which had produced such a great burst of poetry was passing and that the coming social period would be the great age of prose stories and novels. In this he did not think Russia was in any way behind or out of synchronization with Europe. This conviction in the 1840s that the emerging realist novel would be the best vehicle for truthful analysis and radical expression has been maintained by most left critics, including all Communists, ever since.

Consequently Belinskii said little about the small amount of Russian poetry published in 1846. He praised a modern adaptation of *The Tale of the Host of Igor,* said he preferred the original and scoffed at the idea (as he had so often) that it was the greatest work of *Russian* literature. He was most strongly drawn to the volume of poetry of Aleksei Koltsov (1808-1842), the son of a provincial cattle dealer, an humble poet of peasant subjects, language and sensibility, a friend of Belinskii's who had died young four years before. But he had already written a long essay, *On the Life and Works of Koltsov,* and referred readers to that for his detailed opinions. This is one of the problems of the yearly round-up of books; a professional critic has always skimmed the cream of them for separate treatment earlier.

Moving on to prose, Belinskii tells us that only two novels were published in separate editions (i.e. not in journals) in 1846, which surprises us for its revelation of the still primitive state of Russian literature. Belinskii's two and a half pages of discussion of Zagoskin's *Bryansk Forest, an Episode from the Early Years of the Reign of Peter the Great* and the second volume of Butkin's *St. Petersburg Heights* are mixed, convincing and amusing - but we shall never read these books.

At last we come to what we have been waiting for if we know what marked the year 1846 in Russian literature. "Turning to the remarkable works that appeared in story magazines and journals in the past year, our glance, first of all, is caught by *Poor Folk,* a novel which suddenly brought great fame to a previously completely unknown name in literature" (31). But he and many others had written so much about Dostoevskii's first novel earlier in 1846 that he refuses to repeat himself here.

But he is not through with Dostoevskii. "In Russian literature there has never been an example of fame so soon, so quickly won, as the fame of Mr. Dostoevskii. The strength, depth and originality of Mr. Dostoevskii's talent were immediately recognized ..." (32). So far, unalloyed high praise of the kind Dostoevskii delighted in, but the first sour notes were played in the rest of the sentence: "... and, what is still more important, the public immediately ... displayed such an unbounded impatience with his shortcomings as is given only to an uncommon talent" (33).

The following strictures, parts of which are so often quoted to Belinskii's disadvantage, were for the public, but were even more intended as a public exhortation to the talented young novelist, whom Belinskii regarded as having taken the wrong tack after deserved initial success, to return to the main Russian national road.

"Almost everyone found in Mr. Dostoevskii's *Poor Folk* a capacity for tiring the reader even as he admired it, and some attributed this to his garrulity, some to his unrestrained fertility. In fact, it must be conceded that if *Poor Folk* had been one tenth shorter and if the author had had the perspicacity to prune from his novel unnecessary repetitions of phrases and words, his work would have been faultlessly artistic" (34). To us this is *chutzpah*, but a number of sensitive Russian and foreign worshippers of Dostoevskii have said the same thing, if in different tones, of *Poor Folk*.

There is more to come. "In the second issue of *Notes of the Fatherland* Mr. Dostoevskii presented his second novel to the judgment of an interested public, *The Double; the Adventures of Mr. Goliadkin*" (35). This was the most explicit of Dostoevskii's writings on the famous theme of Hoffmann and Gogol, two (or more) characters who share complementary opposite aspects of the same personality and identity, often with overtones of madness and the supernatural. In *The Double*, Goliadkin, a decent but neurotically shy, embarrassed and therefore unsuccessful petty civil servant is confronted by his double, a look-alike with the same name but opposite personality: confident, insinuating, scheming and aggressive, who victoriously usurps the first Goliadkin's place, job and identity, leaving him to be hauled off to the madhouse by a brutal German doctor.

The fantastic element, which Belinskii tolerated without enthusiasm in Gogol, didn't pass muster here. "All the shortcomings in *Poor Folk* which were pardonable in that first attempt appear as immense shortcomings in *The Double*, and they are all included in one: the inability of an excessively rich, strong talent to confine within reasonable measure and boundaries the artistic development of his conceived idea" (36). This isn't specific; Belinskii does then give a specific example of what he meant, not from *The Double* but from Gogol's *Inspector-General*, in which he illustrates Gogol's refusal to repeat himself. The cruel climax of this argument is Belinskii's guess that the novel might have been a success if it had been cut down to at most two thirds of its length. These are ostensibly kindly criticisms intended to help a young author work on a book of solid core-content.

But then Belinskii releases the blade of the guillotine: "But in *The Double* there is still another substantial defect: that is its fantastic coloring. The fantastic, in our time, belongs in madhouses, not in literature, and is the province of doctors,

not of poets" (37). If the "fantastic", Dostoevskii's Hoffmannesque
exploration of the psychic ground that may be madness and may be
supernatural, is cut from *The Double*, its entire subject, concern
and insight into human nature is removed, leaving nothing, a novel
of a category that simply shouldn't have been written. Belinskii
knew perfectly well that *this* was not an helpful, avuncular suggestion but a total rejection. No wonder Dostoevskii's grateful
admiration for Belinskii cooled. No wonder our Dostoevskii-
worshipping literary world's possibility of admiring Belinskii is
aborted.

Considered as a prediction about the literature of "our time",
Belinskii was largely right in the short run; Hoffmannesque fantastic writing by major figures was much rarer in the generation after
1848 than it had been in the previous thirty years. It was a very
poor guess in the long run: Hoffmann, often unrecognized, stands
behind half the giants of Symbolist and Modern writing, painting and
even some of the ballet. The Russian revolutionary tradition and
the Communists have carried these sentiments of Belinskii's in favor
of sanity and realism and against madness and the fantastic up to
the present.

The most significantly influenced person, though, was
Dostoevskii himself. He bristled, flared back and proclaimed his
total resistance to these strictures. But in fact he submitted to
most of Belinskii's demand. Dostoevskii never again invented anything so devilishly supernatural as the appearance of the second
Goliadkin. The possible interventions of Christ in his mature
novels are all constructed so as to alternately read as realistic
natural occurrences. And he never again wrote centrally about what
we call a psychotic – about deeply troubled neurotics who murder and
kill themselves, yes, but never again a paranoid schizophrenic such
as the first Goliadkin.

There is a postscript on Dostoevskii: "In the tenth issue of
Notes of the Fatherland there appeared the third work of Mr.
Dostoevskii, *Mr. Prokharchin*, which came as a disagreeable surprise
to all admirers of Mr. Dostoevskii's talent" (38). This is a story
told with deliberate obscurity of the death of a miser who possessed
a fortune while he lived in disgusting filth in the slums.
Belinskii genuinely found it difficult to follow the story, and
couldn't see that the subject was worth writing on when he did.
"In it glow the hot sparks of a great talent, but they glow in such
dense darkness that they give the reader nothing to see by" (39).
And in this darkness, Belinskii left Dostoevskii for a year.

After this climactic discussion of Dostoevskii, in our view
but not in the work as conceived by Belinskii, it is hard for us to
pay attention to his mixed but often lively and sympathetic accounts
of other Russian tales and novels that appeared in thick journals in
1846, all of which have sunk without a trace. There is a final
four pages on non-fiction, from a translation from the French of
Adolphe Thiers' *History of the Consulate and the Empire* to one
Zhuravskii's *On the Sources and Uses of Statistical Data*. One's
appetite is whetted by his praise of *The Manners, Customs and
Monuments of All Nations of the Globe*, with many magnificent color

plates and woodcuts, the most luxurious book ever published in
Russia, Belinskii thought.

The very nature of this genre of writing, imposed by
Belinskii on himself as an annual duty, would seem to prevent this
work of criticism from being the studied but apparently free-form
work of art that many of his previous essays had been. But this
applies only to the shorter half, the actual catalogue of his views
on works published in 1846. The grand prelude, like some of
Bach's, longer than the fugue, allowed Belinskii to recompose many
of his favorite themes and developments. His unexpectedly respect-
ful critique of the Slavophiles and his thundering affirmation of
personality and nation belong in any anthology of the basic writings
of Belinskii.

CHAPTER 8

"A VIEW OF RUSSIAN LITERATURE IN 1847"

THE last major work written by Belinskii was the second of
his projected series of annual reviews of Russian literature, cut
short by his death, *A View of Russian Literature in 1847*. One can
no longer unthinkingly use the phrase, "written by Belinskii" in
connection with this piece, for he was bedridden for almost all of
the winter of 1847-48 when he produced it in the last phase of his
long illness. He is said to have been able to sit up in bed and
write a good deal of the first part, but the rest of it and all of
the second part was dictated between gasps, chokings and paroxysms
of coughing by a man who could no longer even sit up in bed.

The work's two parts were published in the first and third
issues of the *Contemporary* for 1848. Memoirs testify that they
were read by his many friends in tears, and by many who did not
know Belinskii personally, also in tears, for there were few in the
public who did not know that Belinskii's tragic life was ending.
Belinskii made no explicit mention of his illness in the text - a
self-restraint by no means dictated by Russian custom - and apologized indirectly in it for having failed the public: "The
Contemporary must admit that for reasons entirely beyond the control
of the editors it did not ... fully meet the expectations of the
public in the area of criticism" (1). Practically all readers knew
that Belinskii had written less for the *Contemporary* in 1847 because
tuberculosis had finally overcome him and because he had consented
to make a futile trip to a German spa. The abundance of his
familiar themes, sermons, praises, irritations, tirades and jokes in
the text was simply heart-breaking. Russia was like that in those
days.

The structure invented by Belinskii the year before for this
genre of his writings *was* a kind of Bachian prelude and fugue, an
apparently free-form introduction followed by a more exact catalogue
of the year's writings. This work was about 100 pages long, twice
the length of the earlier survey. Both parts were longer than
before, the second three times longer, and these changes in proportion influenced the tone and effect of the work.

The first installment, Article One, began with an air of
detached meditativeness: "When for a long while no remarkable events

happen which sharply change the ordinary course of things and turn it
in another direction, all the years seem very like each other. But
if a man looks back ... he sees that everything is somehow different
from what it was before" (2). Coming from a man for whom *this* year
was going to be very different from all others - he was obviously
going to die in it - this was unbearable. The first of the original
readers' outbursts of tears must have come here.

Unthinking individuals, "the mass" Belinskii was willing to
call them, judged changes better or worse as if their own cases were
general. But thinking people judge a change not by how it effects
them individually but as a development of society. "Development for
them means going forward, consequently improvement, success,
progress" (3). This *had* to seem to be Belinskii's cry for the only
kind of immortality he believed in: the individual might perish, but
the social progress *this* individual had fought for so doughtily
would sweep on. More tears.

The word "progress" now leads Belinskii to what seems to be
a diversion but what will turn out to be the path to his main theme.
"Our feuilleton writers strongly dislike the word 'progress'" (4).
In Russia as in France at that time, "feuilleton writers" was a code
phrase for conservative pamphleteers. They said they hated it
because it was a foreign word ("*progress*", pronounced, "prah-GRYESS"),
and Belinskii spends two and a half pages mocking linguistic purists
who don't want language to evolve, as he always did. But there is an
elegant play with the language/meta-language paradox here. The
purists don't like the word "progress" because they don't want
language to progress, and they don't want language to progress
because they don't like progress - by which Belinskii clearly meant
political progress. - Still such a strong will to goad the censor,
from a dying man! Moist eyes, but a warm feeling in the heart.

For the last time, Belinskii then preaches his pre-Hegelian
but now Hegelianly phrased conviction that progress is forward movement within a necessary, historically evolving, organically linked,
stage by stage developmental sequence - of a nation's literature, of
a nation's general history, of anything - a thesis with which we are
now very familiar. The problem he attacks here is that this thesis
was not the exclusive property of Hegelian radicals in Russia; the
Slavophiles and court conservatives shared this German Romantic
organic concept, but put it to opposite cultural and political uses.
They even shared Belinskii's view that nations should borrow and
absorb what was organically appropriate for them at a given stage.
All conservatives approved of Russia's absorption of Christianity, as
Belinskii did not, and the non-Slavophile conservatives admired most
of the westernization of Peter and Catherine. Sharing a large
philosophical framework, left and right argued over which innovations and which borrowings were organic and good and which were
indigestible and bad. This was not a philosophical debate but a
political quarrel, and Belinskii was still alive enough to enjoy the
battle to prove that *his* favored literary innovations were necessary,
organic progress, not the reactionaries'. Since we have abandoned
most of our faith in necessary historical and cultural sequences,
and embraced a world of bizarre, contingent, imitations, irruptions
and accidents, we are above this particular battle.

Having set the stage for his main argument, Belinskii warms
up with a last preliminary flourish, a quick round-up of the indis-
putable progress of Russian literature in purely quantitative terms
during the last generation: numbers of books and journals published,
numbers of sales and readers, etc. What strikes us most today are
the statistics of the poverty and primitiveness of the Russian
literary world so short a time before, and even in the 1840s.
Belinskii cites the narrative of Adam Krusenstern, a Baltic baron
who commanded the first Russian expedition to sail around the world,
from 1803 to 1806. Three editions of it were quickly sold out in
advance, literate Germany, even though the Napoleonic Wars were then
raging, while one smaller Russian edition barely sold 200 copies.
This was a splendid illustration of Belinskii's larger point:
Krusenstern's voyage had been a great Russian achievement in foreign-
style ships, just what he thought westernization should do for
Russia. To buy and honor Krusenstern was Western and advanced;
backward-lagging Russia had not even honored itself. Belinskii's
genius for turning anything into a left-right confrontation had a
weird after-echo in America recently, when liberals, in 1980,
finally succeeded in establishing a great Eskimo archaeological site
in Alaska near one of Krusenstern's discoveries as Cape Krusenstern
National Monument, while conservatives opposed it.

Belinskii's main theme is introduced in an apparently negative way, "Strictly speaking, 1847 presented nothing new in literature" (4). Once more he was using words in a peculier Hegelian,
indeed Pickwickian way. He knew that he would say at the beginning
of his actual critical review that 1847 was particularly rich in
remarkable novels, stories and tales. "New" was used very strictly
within his Hegelian theory, where the word meant the next distinct
stage of a well-articulated historical sequence, not additional
examples within the current stage. Belinskii believed that the
current stage of Russian literature, "the natural school", which we
call realism, had triumphed in Gogol in the 1830s, and remained
triumphant. Fine, even great works of the natural school might be
published, but this was a consolidation and deepening of this wonderful stage of Russian literature, nothing *new*.

"The natural school now stands first in Russian literature ...
The public, i.e. the majority of readers, is for it ... Today all
literary activity is concentrated in the journals, and which journals command the greatest reputation, have the widest circle of
readers and the greatest influence on public opinion, but those
which publish the works of the natural school?" (5). It was touch-
ingly modest of the dying man to omit his own major role in bringing
all this about, but he *was*, in these passages, in a determinist mood
which denied anything so accidental as individual human input.

An abbreviated ghost of one of Belinskii's accustomed surveys
of the whole history of Russian literature leads at once to a discussion of Gogol, the founding hero of the natural school. When
Gogol emerged in the 1830s, Belinskii remembered, his enemies were
members of the rhetorical school. His vagueness in discussing them
enables him to hint that they were political as well as cultural
rightists, and that the young Gogol was a left wing figure. But now
the cultural right was the Slavophiles, and they too hailed Gogol as

the founder and great figure of Russian realism. This was good, Belinskii thought, for it showed that realism was now the national consensus, but of course he argued that the Slavophiles were all wrong in claiming Gogol for their own.

He now appropriates some praise of Gogol by a conservative critic, one Vasilii Plaksin. The fellow is confused, Belinskii sneers, but he recognizes the outstanding qualities of Gogol, originality and independence. Zhukovskii had been influenced by the Germans and Pushkin by Byron, "But Gogol had no models, there were no predecessors either in Russian or in foreign literatures" (6). Communists still maintain this while foreign scholars argue the influence of Sterne, Hoffmann and others. Belinskii's ideology did not force him to deny foreign predecessors of Gogol; he was the great apostle of fruitful borrowing. A genuine dazzled admiration swept Belinskii into his intense conviction of Gogol's genius-like originality..

It had to be explained somehow, in fact and according to Belinskii's scheme of things. "All the works of Gogol are concerned exclusively with representing the world of Russian life, and he has no rivals in the art of portraying it in all its truth" (7). In spite of Belinskii's determined internationalist nationalism, this more Slavophile side comes out from time to time. Gogol's marvelous portrayal of *Russian* truth could not have been inspired by a foreigner. An earlier Russian, of course, might have shown Russia truthfully. Belinskii had written a whole book to show that Pushkin had done so. But now that he is dealing with Gogol, Belinskii will say what he never said when writing on Pushkin himself: "Gogol ... never softens or embellishes for the sake of ideals or preconceived ideas or some customary bias, as, for example, Pushkin did in *Onegin*, where he idealized the landlords' existence" (8). This passage sounds as if "idealization" meant conservative whitewash, and so it did for Belinskii, but that was only part of it.

A far older cultural meaning of idealization is implied here, the aesthetically (not politically) motivated process of making things more beautiful than they are. This is why Belinskii keeps contrasting older, idealized literary works with Gogol's *truth*. Truth is not ugliness in contrast to idealized beauty; truth is everything that is - beauty, ugliness, goodness, evil and all other qualities mixed up together - in contrast to the careful selection of beauty alone. No broadly truthful depiction can be wholly beautiful, but something much better, truth itself - an end in itself and a means to move society forward as pure beauty never can be.

Belinskii believed that Gogol presented *all* that was there in Russia, not choosing according to aesthetic or any other theory. He praised Gogol for being *unselective* in his Russian subject matter, not in the sense of having no taste or control, but in the sense of deliberately excluding no category of Russian reality. Belinskii never mentioned the developing art of photography, which he would certainly have loved had he lived long enough to encounter it. But what he valued in Gogol here was remarkably parallel to the non-selective and non-exclusive West European paintings of Gogol's lifetime and the early photographs made in accordance with the same realist non-aesthetic aesthetic, which have been rediscovered for us by Peter Galassi's important exhibition in 1981 at New York's Museum of Modern Art, and book, *Before Photography*. If this was Gogol's technique, Belinskii could only repeat phrases such as "amazing truth and fidelity to reality", to convey his impression, as did many contemporary viewers of early photography. These were parts of a broad sentiment and trend of the 1840s.

Shortly after this climax of his last great panegyric to Gogol, he comments, "After *Dead Souls* Gogol wrote nothing" (9), and suddenly we remember things with a jolt. Gogol had indeed written and published something, his *Selected Passages from Correspondence with Friends*, which Belinskii was to mention with icy brevity in the second half of this survey. The previous July Belinskii had written his *Letter to Gogol*, which was already gaining an underground fame, in which he utterly blasted poor Gogol for having deserted the realist and progressive cause. To write *this* five months after the *Letter* was not an act of concealment, diplomacy or even politeness, for this was the fanatically truthful Belinskii. It was an obituary for the truly great Gogol, who was still physiologically alive but who, by Belinskii's standards, was no more.

With Gogol morally dead, his "school" was left to continue realism in Russian literature. Belinskii could praise some of them to the skies when reviewing them, but when he thought of them in connection with Gogol, he judged them all, even Turgenev and Dostoevskii, to be epigonal. They will be discussed in the second article. Now he refutes an argument often heard in Russia – and in Europe – against realism as such.

He says the rhetorical (meaning reactionary) carpers claim that realist writers write on subjects and characters which were not lofty, noble and inspiring, as literature should be, and which therefore have a negative and even immoral effect on the public. This was of course the tail end of a grand theory of literature and culture with a tremendous Classical, Renaissance and Neoclassical pedigree. But it was also weighed down by snobbery, and Belinskii at first belittles it by reducing it to the demand for prettified shepherdesses in French Eighteenth Century masques. He rises to seriousness again by insisting that truth and fidelity to reality are nobler virtues than beauty or moral exhortation. To fend off Nicholas's censorship, the language is abstract here, but it is highly probable that Belinskii was arguing that beauty and moral exhortation urge us on to personal improvement, as conservatives want, without touching social institutions, but truth and fidelity to reality show us *all* of our defects, the most important part of which is our complicity in the evils of society, and thereby impel us to radical reform of self *and* society. This was both less and more than our own view of the virtue of realism, that it confronts us with our own existential nature and the human condition – but without any direct political consequence.

He then returns to putting snobbery down. Too many objectors to realism are *nouveau-riches* who don't want to be reminded of the low origins from which they had recently risen. As a *raznochinets*,

Belinskii surely knew the foibles of his less noble fellow-
raznochintsy. He turns on upper class aesthetic snobs, too. Nature
is the eternal model for art. The coarse and uneducated *muzhik* is
just as human and should be just as interesting to an analyst of
humanity as an educated nobleman. Isn't the organism of a savage
Australian as worthwhile for an anatomist to study as that of a
civilized European? Does a botanist scorn wild species and study
only highly cultivated plants? and the mocking clincher: the
Redeemer came into the world for all men: he chastised the rich and
the educated and comforted the poor, the toilers, the sick, the
filthy and the fallen. With delightful wickedness, Belinskii drafts
Christ for the radical democratic cause and goes as far as he can to
represent His mission on earth as an earlier social equivalent of
the realist novel. If so, conservative anti-realists would have to
give over the attack.

Belinskii then turns to blasting the proponents of pure art,
a position that overlaps what he had just rejected. Since pure art
is a concept usually advanced in the visual arts, it enabled
Belinskii, at the close of his career, to make his only really important statement about a painting. He was not arguing with French
partisans of *l'art pour l'art*, artists and aesthetes who felt that
artistic creations need serve no outside purpose but were high ends
in themselves, as objects and as a way of life. He was launching
into what he called "dreamy Germans" (and their Russian followers)
who thought that pure, unconditional, absolute art could raise our
souls high above this merely earthly, human, muddy world of
particulars.

Belinskii hotly denied that there was or could be any such
pure art divorced from the particulars of this world. In his argument Belinskii had the immense advantage of living in age when all
finished painting was still entirely representational, so that
arguments that there could be "pure" and what was then called
"abstract" art (unparticularized subjects, such as unidentifiable
nudes) made problems for artistic people as well as for Philistines.
The very word in Russian for painting, *zhivopis'*, refers not to the
medium, as the English and French words do, but means "life-write".
Arguments for pure abstract art become consistent only when there
is our kind of abstract art to argue for.

He briefly cited the most prestigious Russian painter then
alive, Karl Briullov (1799-1852). His celebrated portraits, which
were never of *muzhiks* and were in no way radical appeals, were
nevertheless of the highest fidelity to nature and teach us much
about mankind. Relapsing into literature, he maintained that
Shakespeare, Milton and Walter Scott were unpolitical or conservative writers, but their works contain enormous quantities of
extremely truthful portrayals of the world.

These were non-political artists, not artists who were supposed to be divorced from the particulars of this world. "We said
that pure, abstract, unconditional, or as philosophers say, *absolute*
art never existed anywhere. If anything of the sort could have
existed, it might have been the works of art of those epochs in
which art was the chief interest, the exclusive concern of the

most educated class of society. Such, for instance, were the works of the painters of the Italian schools of the Sixteenth Century. Their content, apparently, is prevailingly religious; but that is for the most part a mirage, and in fact the subject of these paintings is beauty as beauty, more in the plastic or classical sense of the word than the romantic" (10).

This is not how we would discuss High Renaissance art. Belinskii had never been to Italy. He had earlier boasted that he had made a thorough study of the paintings and sculptures on public view in the Hermitage in St. Petersburg, a much smaller collection than is visible today, but already rich in Italian art. And on his desperate trip to Germany and France for his health the previous summer, he made partial visits to the Dresden Painting Gallery and to the Louvre. So he was able to say, as if offhandedly, "Take, for example, the Madonna of Raphael, this *chef d-oeuvre* of Italian painting in the Sixteenth Century" (11).

This, *the* Madonna of Raphael to any Nineteenth Century Russian, was his *Sistine Madonna* (See the plate on the next page). It was painted by Raphael at some disputed time between 1513 and 1516 and installed as a papal benefaction in the Church of San Sisto (the sainted Pope Sixtus II) in Piacenza, either by the heirs of Pope Julius II or by the then Pope Leo X. In 1754 it was bought for an irresponsibly gigantic sum by Augustus II, Elector of Saxony and King of Poland from 1733 to 1763, and installed in his opulent collection in Dresden. From that moment it was the pride of the Saxon court and became the greatest and most important painting in the world for Russian travelers, who usually saw Dresden before any other major art center of Europe. It was tremendously admired by Central and West Europeans too, but for them it shared the pinnacle with other masterpieces; for most Russians it stood alone.

Belinskii's procedure, in beginning this, his famous discussion of the *Sistine Madonna*, was to invoke the most notable Russian panegyric on it, written in the 1820s by the celebrated poet Zhukovskii. "Who does not remember Zhukovskii's article about this superb work, who from his youth has not formed his idea of it from this article? Who then did not believe the unassailable truth that this work is preeminently romantic, that the face of the Madonna is the highest ideal of that unearthly beauty, which secretly reveals itself only to the inner contemplation, and that only in rare moments of pure, triumphant inspiration?" (12).

The first sentence was true at the time. The second burlesques Zhukovskii's quite sufficiently rhapsodic paean, and makes it thunderingly clear that Belinskii does not believe it. The axe will fall. "The author of the present article recently saw this picture" (13).

We are extraordinarily lucky to have three versions of how he responded to it. Pavel Annenkov was taking care of Belinskii during his week in Dresden, and wrote in his *Literary Reminiscences* that, "He would stroll listlessly along the bank of the Elbe, looked at the city without interest, went to the Green Vaults [the incredible museum of the piled-up jeweled confections of the Saxon kings] whose expensive children's toys and treasures roused his attention with the effect of making him almost angry, and finally visited the Picture Gallery twice. There, as tourists ordinarily do, he sat in front of the *Sistine Madonna,* but he came away with an impression completely contrary to the one they usually experience there and later write down. He was the first, it seems, not to go into an ecstasy over her celestial tranquility and equanimity, but on the contrary to be horrified by her ..." (14)   "In the Dresden gallery he underwent another aesthetic trial: he came to that little *chef d'oeuvre* of Rubens, *The Judgment of Paris* .... Belinskii, accustomed to think of Venus and Greek woman.as embodiments of ideal beauty on earth, found himself there in front of three naked matrons .... Realism in painting aroused revulsion in the partisan of realism in literature" (15).

Then we have a four page fragment of Belinskii's own letter from Dresden to Vasilii Botkin, dated July 19 (New Style), 1847, so we can contrast his early and private thoughts on this great painting to his later public formulation. "I went to the Dresden gallery and saw Raphael's *Madonna.* What nonsense the romantics wrote about her, especially Zhukovskii. To me there is nothing either romantic or classical about her face. This isn't the mother of the Christian God: this is an aristocratic woman, the daughter of a tsar, *idéal sublime du comme il faut* [sublime ideal of propriety] . She looks at us, well, not with scorn – that wouldn't become her, she is too well bred to hurt anyone, even the common people; she doesn't look at us as *canailles* [rabble] : that word would be too coarse and impure for her noble lips; no, she looks at us with frigid favor, fearing the taint of our look but unwilling to annoy us plebeians by turning away. The child she holds in her arms is more frank; in him one can find a slight but proud wrinkle of the lower lip, his whole mouth expresses contempt for us *racailles* [trash] . In his eyes we don't see the future god of love, peace, forgiveness and salvation, but rather the Old Testament God of wrath and fury, of vengeance and punishment. But what nobility, what delicacy of the brush! It's impossible to admire it sufficiently! I couldn't help recalling Pushkin .... No wonder Pushkin was so fond of Raphael; they were kindred natures" (16). The only other painting in Dresden Belinskii mentioned in this letter was a *Leda and the Swan,* then listed as by Michelangelo. "I very much liked Michelangelo's picture of Leda at the moment of intercourse with the swan; to say nothing about her body (especially *les fesses* [the buttocks]) the pain and distress of ecstasy are imprinted on her face with amazing power" (17). Apparently Belinskii was not so much shocked by realistic sex in painting as Annenkov was led to believe.

Finally, in *A View of Russian Literature in 1847,* printed six months later, Belinskii's text dwells on how profoundly he had been moved so long ago by reading Zhukovskii's description of the *Sistine Modonna.* Continuing as the third person "author", he says, "Twice he went to the Dresden Gallery and both times he saw only this picture, even when he was looking at others or when he wasn't looking at anything" (18). What? No Venus? No Leda? No *fesses*? "But the longer and more intently he looked at that picture, the more he thought then and the more he was convinced later that the Madonna of Raphael and the Madonna described by Zhukovskii under the

Belinskii's home

inskii just before his death. (painted by A. Naumov)
m left: Nekrasov, Belinskii, Panaev, Mariia (wife of Belinskii),daughter Ol'ga.

"Madonna Sistina" by Raefael

name of Raphael are two completely different pictures" (19). This
was to smash one of the public's idols, Zhukovskii, and to give
thrilling promise of an assault on a greater idol, Raphael.

"The Madonna of Raphael is a severely classical figure and
not at all romantic" (20). In the letter to Botkin it was the *face*
that was neither Romantic *nor* Classical. "Her face expresses that
beauty which exists independently, not drawing its charm from any
moral expression in the face. To that face, on the contrary,
nothing can be attributed" (21). This suggests another meaning of
"pure art", no more attractive to Belinskii than the others. The
face of the Madonna, like her whole figure, possesses inexpressible
nobility and dignity. It is the daughter of a tsar, aware of her
high rank and personal dignity. In her look is something severe and
restrained, not gentle or kind, not proud and contemptuous .... It
might be called the *idéal sublime du comme il faut*. There is no
shadow of the illusive, the mysterious, the misty or the glimmering,
in a word, of the romantic; on the contrary, in everything there is
such a distinct, clear definiteness, a finality, such a severe
regularity and faithfulness of feature and together with that such a
noble, masterful brush!" (22). Belinskii certainly put his finger on
the fact that Raphael was not a Northern painter.

"Religious contemplation in this picture is expressed only in
the face of the divine child, but a contemplation exclusively particular to the Catholicism of the time. In the posture of the child,
in the hands stretched out to those in front ... in the dilated
pupils of the eyes are expressed anger and menace, and in the raised
lower lip a proud contempt. This is not the God of forgiveness and
gentleness, not the lamb who bears the sins of the world; this is
the God who judges and punishes. From this it is evident that there
is nothing romantic in the figure of the child ... Rather, only in
the faces of the angels, distinguished by an unusual expression of
intelligence and soulfully contemplating the appearance of divinity,
can one find anything romantic" (23).

Neither Belinskii's letter nor his article express the horror
of the Madonna which Annenkov thought he saw. The letter to Botkin
is much breezier than the dignified passage in the article. It is
also more negative about Catholic concepts of Christ, and much more
enthusiastic about Raphael's icy skill, which is noticed but not
compared to Pushkin's in the article. This is the end of Belinskii's
discussion of the *Sistine Madonna*. He has told why he doesn't think
it Romantic, and has clearly indicated why he doesn't think it pure,
abstract art in the German Romantic sense, although he didn't
explicitly conclude this argument at the end.

To us this is a strange, unmodern discussion of a painting.
There is nothing about the circumstances of its creation, save the
doubtful implication that Raphael was living in a Catholic atmosphere
like that of Inquisitorial Spain, nothing of the harmonious pyra-
midal composition, nothing of the studied scheme of colors, nothing
about the scene – literally a cloud of angels – or the framing cur-
tains, no iconography in our sense, not even a mention of Saint
Barbara on the right, an actual princess far more elegantly dressed
and sniffy than the Madonna, or of Saint Sixtus on the left, to us

the outstanding figure of the painting, with his magnificent papal robe, brow, nose and whiskers.

Even for the 1840s these were clearly the impressions of a literary man living in a verbal universe, not of an artist. He noticed the Christ child's extended hands but not his crossed legs, and not the interaction of the carrying mother and the carried child. When we guess the intended emotions in painted faces which are not obviously laughing or being crucified, we submit ourselves to a Rorschach test. Belinskii's interpretations were and are a minority report. He found the two *putti* below soulful and Romantic; all Germans and most others have thought they are overpoweringly cute real six year old boys. Scholars have missed the royal aloofness Belinskii saw so plainly in the Madonna, and have failed to notice the contempt and hellfire in the child.

But Belinskii did speak to his generation of Russians. He succeeded in smashing the idol Zhukovskii had built into the painting. Most Russians who commented on the *Sistine Madonna* after 1848, including Turgenev and Tolstoi, but not Dostoevskii, noted and rejected Zhukovskii's interpretation in favor of Belinskii's. James Billington, in his thoughtful essay, *The Missing Madonna*, in his *The Icon and the Axe*, suggests that these Russians, consciously or unconsciously, wanted the technically primitive but emotional and supportive Russian Madonna of the icons which they felt they had lost, realizing it with a pang when faced with Raphael's Europe-symbolizing, cold perfection. This is most likely of Tolstoi and possibly of Turgenev, but Belinskii had a different temperament. It really was medieval Catholicism he rejected, not all of progressive Europe. He preferred forgiving and gentle representations of God, but not out of any ache for a lost, all-encompassing Orthodox faith; they were more in line with the humane, secular society of the future which was his conscious and, if he had any, unconscious emotional core.

The rest of the first article is a falling action. Greek art, Goethe and (again) Shakespeare were not "pure" but had national settings. For a final metaphor he quoted Nekrasov's completely Belinskian editorial in the first issue of the refounded *Contemporary*, comparing Russian literature a short while before to the early Russian spring when grass sprang on some hills but the gullies were still full of blackened snow and mud; now the green carpet, though not yet brilliant, covers everything, and the finest flowery season of the year is approaching. He ended the first article with the word he had begun by justifying so vigorously: "We think that in this there is progress" (24).

*   *   *

The second installment, Article Two, begins with its own prelude, Belinskii's last notable ode, along lines quite familiar to us, to the advancing age of prose. "The novel and the story, even when they depict the most ordinary and banal prose of everyday existence, can be examples of the uttermost limits of art" (25).

Now he launches into the actual view of Russian literature in 1847. Now he says, "Last, year, 1847, was particularly rich in remarkable novels, stories and tales. For formidable success with the public, first place belongs to two novels, *Who is to Blame?* and *An Ordinary Story*" (26).

The chance of this pairing forced or allowed Belinskii, in his last campaign, to write at length on the problem we want to shake him with, and all his successors, art versus message, for it just so happened that *Who is to Blame?* is a type-example of the famous Russian problem, novel, thoughtful, humane and progressive, but not outstandingly crafted, while *An Ordinary Story* is a beautifully crafted work, detached, even icy, with no political tendency at all.

Who is to Blame? may be the last important Russian novel to be translated in English -- only in 1985. Belinskii begins his twelve page discussion by telling us everything about the writings of its author, "Mr. Iskander" (the Persian and Turkish for Alexander), except the important things, which Nicholas's censorship made it impossible to print. For "Iskander" was the pseudonym of Aleksandr Herzen, Belinskii's true Russian friend, co-founder and leader with him of the loose Westerner movement, Russia's first socialist, twice arrested and exiled for subversion, who had in January, 1847, used a temporary traveler's passport illegally to escape with his family from Russia to Paris, where he became the leader of the Russian revolutionary exiles and whence he fired back many revolutionary salvos against the Russian slave state.

The cluster of problems in *Who is to Blame?* is stirringly feminist: how can a really strong, able, autonomous woman live in Nicholas's Russia, or indeed anywhere in the Nineteenth Century world? How can she escape the dependency she was born into? How can she be the wife of a husband who is decent but vastly inferior to her? How should she manage when she later meets and loves a man more worthy of her mettle? *Who is to Blame?*, Belinskii notes, was the first Russian novel derived from the radical and feminist novels of George Sand. It was the chief predecessor of Chernyshevskii's overpoweringly influential socialist and feminist novel of 1863, *What is to be Done?*

Herzen had his heroine, ironically, called "Liubon'ka", the diminutive of a Russian girl's name meaning "love". She marries the not at all ironically named Krutsiferskii ("Cross-bearer"), a kind and decent idealist who is neither bright nor effective and whom both Herzen and Belinskii call a "child", meaning an adolescent character. It is made very clear that "Krutsiferskii did not marry; he was married", in spite of warnings that Liubon'ka was "a *tiger cub* that still *doesn't know its own strength*" (27). Herzen's "tiger cub" was more appropriate and admiring than the later Symbolists' term, "*femme fatale*". Krutsiferskii is a highly contented husband for four years while Liubon'ka, as we can tell from passages in her diary, slowly becomes conscious of her dissatisfaction caused by their inequality of character. In the second half of the novel she becomes close to and loves Bel'tov, a strong-minded, active and restless *intelligent*. In both life and realist fiction in the 1840s, love outside of marriage had to end tragically and does so, in spite of the highmindedness and decency of everyone involved. Who is to blame? Herzen was not the sort to give a simple-minded answer, a simple villain or a simple caricature of a repressive society. Instead he shows that it was caused by complex and indefinable elements in all the three leading characters, and by the tragic contradiction that society has to enforce stable marriage even at great human cost.

Belinskii's critical view is a strange one to us: Herzen is not a bad writer of fiction, but he is no poet. Many scenes and characters are effective, but the presentation of the chief charac-ters, Liubon'ka and Bel'tov, has serious weaknesses and in Bel'tov's case inconsistencies. But the ideas, the thought and the exposition of the concept of humanity in the novel are extraordinary and make the novel as a whole outstanding.

In our normal contemptuous Western rejection of Russian revolutionary fiction and criticism - of Belinskii, Chernyshevskii, Gorkii and the Communists, our main theme is that the Russian radi-cals wanted and wrote pamphlets under the guise of fiction, in which complex, life-like characters and situations were precluded by omni-present ideology, and that they all thought omnipresence of ideology was the only quality of good fiction. And the defense by the few Westerners who see more than that in left Russian fiction also assumes all modern Western critical values: No, the best left Russian fiction was less ideological and more life-like than is often realized.

How different was Belinskii's actual critical stance and criticism! He was perfectly aware of Herzen's weaknesses (but by no means failure) "as a novelist" we would say: Belinskii's phrase was "as a poet". "To see the author of *Who is to Blame?* as an unusual artist is a complete misunderstanding of his talent ... His chief strength is not creativity or artistry but thought, profoundly worked out, fully conscious and developed" (28). The story of the tragic love is well told, but not artistically told. The spoiled, impractical Bel'tov of the first half of the novel is replaced in the second half by Bel'tov the genius at loss in our society. A number of the minor characters are fine. The book isn't really a novel but a series of biographies. It is an idea which makes the novel great. "What is this idea? It is suffering, pain at the sight of unrecognized human dignity ... It is what the Germans call 'humanity.'"(29). There follows a page and a half of what it means to treat fellow human beings with humanity - apparently the first sustained analysis in Russian of this now so common idea.

This is a critical position which we find incomprehensible and maddening. Belinskii easily accepts all our aesthetic and for-mal demands on a novel - language, structure, character and the rest - after all, he had *always* promoted them. He gives Herzen's novel the same mixture of 'B's and 'D's by this set of criteria that we would give it. But Belinskii has another set of criteria: soundness, originality and progressiveness of thought - we may call it ideology if we want, which he thinks equally important for a novel. He *knows* Herzen is not the poetic novelist that Gogol is, but he also knows that Gogol is not the philosophical novelist Herzen is. Both deserve 'A's for their respective strengths, and nowhere will Belinskii say that either set of these criteria is more important for a work of literature than the other. He admires both and hopes that in the near future both will be combined in many masterworks.

Here we differ. We are utterly convinced that the "creative", "artistic" basket of criteria for good literature, the gradient from language through character, is the sole standard. Thought, progressive or otherwise, is all very well, but simply not the main point of literature. We, who freely accuse the Russian left of having one, narrow, ideological standard for literature, in fact insist on one standard and one alone, while Belinskii was a pluralist.

We can not share his spirit and play his critical game. He proves that he can play ours in his immediately following treatment of the other novel of this pair, *An Ordinary Story*, the first novel of Ivan Goncharov (1812-1891). This and Belinskii's other champion-ing reviews of it constituted his last discovery of a major Russian writer in the bud. We know Goncharov, as Belinskii never could, for his second novel, published in 1856, *Oblomov*, the greatest study of sloth in world literature, which famously begins with the hero tak-ing seventy five pages to get out of bed. This absolute masterpiece has unfortunately eclipsed *An Ordinary Story*, even in Russia.

Goncharov's novel was the first major Russian variant on the great French theme of Stendhal and Balzac, the young provincial with Romantic ideas who goes to the capital to experience the world, to blunder in it and to become progressively disillusioned. In this case, the young man, Aduev, is considerably more "ordinary" than Julien Sorel, Eugène de Rastignac or Lucien Chardon. He has Romantic notions rather than ideas. He blunders away all chances of a successful career and the loves of two attractive women, and returns, a wreck, to his dismal provincial home. In contrast, the other great character of the novel, Aduev's uncle Pëtr Ivanich, had been successful in St. Petersburg, had made an advantageous marriage, had ruined his wife's life not by cruelty but by being incapable of fulfilling her love, and had built a great void for himself within.

Belinskii devotes twenty two pages to *An Ordinary Story*, much of it a précis of the plot. His comments are mostly on the order of, how true! how very frequent and ordinary this story is! how delicately rendered! how terribly true! He particularly praises the many portraits of women in the book, mostly weak or nasty women. Belinskii's overall judgment is highly admiring but also a little queasy. "A complete contrast to [Herzen] is presented by the author of *An Ordinary Story*. He is a poet, an artist and nothing more. He has neither love nor enmity for the characters created by him, they give him neither joy nor anger, and he gives no moral lessons, either to them or to the reader. He seems to think, if you get into trouble, it's up to you to get out of it and none of my affair. Of all contemporary writers he and he alone approaches the

ideal of pure art ..." (30). Such detachment was appropriate in
Pushkin's day, but is divorced from its time now in 1847. Besides,
Pushkin was never so wholly icy! But "Mr. Goncharov's novel is one
of the remarkable works of Russian literature" (31).

Belinskii's critical balance was severely tested by *An
Ordinary Story*. It had all of one set of the literary virtues in
his theory and none of the other. The pluralism of his theory dictated that this was sufficient ground to judge it a fine work, and
he consistently did so - but it obviously left him cold. Herzen's
novel leaned to the other side, but less lopsidedly, and Belinskii
really warmed to it. Can we condemn Belinskii for drawing back from
what did not coincide with his ideology and sympathies, though he
did not fall over backwards? Or *was* Goncharov at this early stage
just a cold fish? Since formal virtues were this novel's all,
Belinskii severely criticized its inconsistent epilogue (in which
Aduev returns to St. Petersburg and succeeds in both career and
marriage), while he was gentle with such faults in Herzen. The
reserved Goncharov seems to have listened. He worked very slowly.
Nine years later, *Oblomov* displayed no inconsistencies, and gave
Russia its great, heart-warming national anti-hero.

There are a number of brief notices in the remaining lesser
half of Article Two. The most touching is Belinskii's praise for
the first parts of *Dombey and Son* - he had always loved Dickens,
though he hadn't "discovered" him - and he wished that the rest of it
would soon be translated into Russian, which he never lived to see.
The last section gives his last treatment of three giants.

"We should now deal with *A Sportsman's Sketches* of Mr.
Turgenev" (32). Four pages deal with the four stories published in
1847 of what would eventually become a set of twenty four.
Belinskii recalled Turgenev's earlier narrative poems, but concludes
that Turgenev has found his real path in narrative prose. Without
detailing why, he praised *Khor and Kalinych*, which stands first in
complete editions of *A Sportsman's sketches*, as an absolute gem, and
that has been the judgment of posterity. After this, it seems like
quite a putdown for Belinskii to have written, "Evidently [Turgenev]
does not have a talent for pure creation, he can not create characters ... He can depict reality he has seen and studied, create,
if you want, but only out of ready, given materials of reality" (33).
This is a textbook application of a Kantian distinction, but it
seems insufferably condescending to Turgenev. Yet at the time and
at moments in later life, this was the diffident Turgenev's judgment
of his own abilities. They were close friends; one wonders which of
them, in conversation, had first suggested this view to the other.
The four pages finish with, "It is impossible not to wish that Mr.
Turgenev will write whole volumes of such stories" (34). Five years
later the still grieving Turgenev was to record that the encouragement and the memory of Belinskii had inspired him to do so.

Two witty pages devastate Dostoevskii's story of 1847, *The
Landlady*, a Hoffmannesque tale in which a scientist, Ordinov falls
under the spell of a bewitching lady who has a sinister husband.
"Odd scenes follow: the merchant's wife talks nonsense, of which we
don't understand one single word, but Ordinov listened to her and

constantly fell into faints .... What they said to each other to
make them wave their hands, grimace, break things, swoon, recover,
take leave of their senses, we surely don't know, for of all those
long, pathetic monologues we don't understand one word" (35).
This wicked and deliberate incomprehension was the last stage of
Belinskii's disillusionment with Dostoevskii.

Belinskii concluded his *View of Russian Literature in 1847*
with a far deadlier blow at what he regarded as far greater quarry:
"Last year the attention of the critics was predominantly devoted to
The Correspondence of Gogol with his Friends [a farcical mistitling].
One can say that the memory of this book is now preserved only in
the articles about it" (36). Period.

So ended Belinskii's last sustained work. It was read then
and should be now with full knowledge of the author's dying body.
But it shows no decline whatsoever in his powers as a reader and a
discoverer, as a friend and a bastard, as a critic and writer, or
as he would like to have put it, as a thinker and a poet.

CHAPTER   9

THE LETTER TO GOGOL

BELINSKII'S letter to Gogol of July 3, 1847, is certainly the most widely printed, read, memorized, famous and influential piece the great critic and crusader ever wrote. *Belinskii's Letter to Gogol*, as it is almost always called, is regarded as his greatest work and his testament, and as one of the great documents of the Russian revolutionary movement. It is often called the most important letter in Russian history, sometimes even in world history. The *Letter* is usually described as the summarizing climax of the thoughts and feelings of the revolutionaries of the reign of Nicholas I, and as the most direct and moving stimulus to the much wider revolutionary movement of the following reign of Alexander II – and in a more distant way, to the later phases of the Russian revolution, and to foreign movements everywhere.

This is a great deal of freight to load on one letter which takes up only ten to fifteen pages in printed editions, and which really was a letter written from one person to another, and not a book in epistolary form, such as Burke's *Reflections on the Late Revolution in France*. The *Letter* is usually said to have been poured forth molten, a chaotic cascade of Belinskii's wonderful wrath. I believe that it has been effective in part because of its skilfully composed formal structure. Like so many of Belinskii's major writings, it has the fluid and complex form of a contemporary piece of Romantic music, in this case a discernible introduction, exposition, development with variations and recapitulation.

I shall also submit a minority report about its content. The *Letter* indeed contains the anti-tsarist blasts and emancipating revolutionism it is famous for, but in its main exposition it does not set forth a revolutionary view of politics but a surprisingly Protestant view of personal relations and of religion. I suggest that part of the *Letter*'s great importance is precisely that it is a classic exposition of these Protestant views which are among the core convictions of most modern revolutionaries.

The story of how Belinskii wrote his *Letter to Gogol* has not only been told often; it is *always* told. It is part of every account of Russian politics and literature. It is an absolutely classic Russian anecdote.

After Gogol reached his acme with the publication of the first part of *Dead Souls* in 1842, his always divided self split further, and he sank into a permanent psychological crisis, which prevented the completion of *Dead Souls* and took an increasingly religious form. From 1836 on, after the blow-up at the first performances of *The Inspector General*, Gogol lived abroad, in Rome and other cities, out of direct touch with Belinskii. The latter hoped for a magnificent continuation of *Dead Souls*, but feared, from the reports of friends and from at least one article by Gogol, *Odyssey*, that he was turning religious, mystical and reactionary.

In 1846 Gogol sent to Russia the manuscript of his last book, *Selected Passages from Correspondence with Friends*, which was presently published and forthwith became a major literary scandal. It was not a work of fiction but a series of leisurely - many said wandering - didactic essays in the guise of letters. Some set forth Gogol's views of literature and aesthetics, but nobody paid any attention to them. Most were on moral-social-political themes, imbued with a strong and somewhat unorthodox Orthodox Christianity. The book was certainly not just tsarist propaganda, much less bureaucratic-reactionary. "Conservative-Slavophile" is perhaps the best classification for this unclassifiable and fascinating work. But the book was certainly for the Tsar rather than for revolution, for moral Christian personal life rather than for public political effort, very much for the established Orthodox Church and its privileges that were then under fire, and, in selected passages, for serfdom and traditional serf obedience to landlords, against literacy for serfs, and for censorship and police arrest of radical dissenters.

The *intelligentsia* were at first staggered - this??? - from the author of *Dead Souls?* - and then enraged at the man they now regarded as a traitor, for Gogol had been wrongly judged to have been himself a revolutionary *intelligent*, prevented from saying so in his stories only by Nicholas's censorship. The rage was not easy to express in print, for the censors, though undelighted by Gogol in any of his transformations, were not going to let this un-asked-for support be undermined. Belinskii wrote a long article against Gogol's book in the *Contemporary*, which appeared early in 1847, but self-censorship and on this tense occasion censorship in the editor's office, even before official censorship, had reduced it to something very abstract and bland for the man known as Raging Vissarion. Belinskii apologized for this emasculation to friends such as Botkin: "I had to act against my nature and character. Nature wants me to bark like a dog and howl like a jackal,but circumstances force me to mew like a cat and wag my tail like a fox" (1).

But Russians were long since past masters at reading between the lines, and Gogol may have been having a nervous breakdown, but he was no fool. He had the publisher and editor of the *Contemporary* forward a letter to Belinskii, if they thought he might be receptive. They could not have thought that, but they forwarded the letter. It reached him near the middle of the West European July, 1847, at the spa of Salzbrunn in Prussian Silesia, where Belinskii was taking the waters so useless against his now galloping consumption.

Gogol thought that Belinskii was offended by his passages against unnamed radical journalistic critics who were gaining such a large and baleful influence lately. It is hard to see how this could have meant anyone but Belinskii. Gogol's letter was filled with Christian good will, soft answers to turn away wrath, meekness and kindness - always infuriating to Belinskii. "I was grieved to read your article about me ... I didn't mind the damning attack on me in public, but it seemed like the voice of a man who is angry at me. I don't want to make even a stranger angry at me, much less you, whom I have always thought of as a man who loves me. I never wanted to pain you in a single passage in my book. I can't understand now why I have provoked the anger of every last man in Russia" (2).

The omnipresent Annenkov was in the room at Salzbrunn when Belinskii read Gogol's letter. According to his *Literary Reminiscences*, Belinskii turned red and burst out, "Aha! He doesn't understand why people are angry at him ; it'll have to be explained to him - I'll answer him!". And for the next three mornings, after coming back from the waters, Belinskii worked at his reply, stimulated by coffee, until he had to stop work for the day at lunch. Annenkov noted that Belinskii was composing not just a private letter, but a document for the public, and of course three days of writing and lying in bed gave him plenty of time to plan and polish the *Letter to Gogol*.

When Belinskii finished it, he read the *Letter* aloud to Annenkov, who was both admiring and worried. "I was apprehensive about both the substance and tone of the reply - naturally not for Belinskii's sake...". Annenkov, in mid-1847, didn't yet fear that Nicholas's police would intercept letters by Russians in foreign countries; that would begin only the next year, after the revolutions of 1848. "I was apprehensive for Gogol's sake, who was going to get this letter. I could imagine his feelings the moment he began to read this terrible indictment". Several copies must have been made before the *Letter*, which was dated July 3 (Old Style), 1847, was entrusted to the super-efficient Prussian post on the Western July 15, for Annenkov had at least two copies, one of which he gave shortly afterwards to the equally omnipresent Herzen, who was even more admiring and not a bit worried about Gogol. Annenkov remembers that Herzen, deeply moved, murmured, "It is a work of genius, and, I believe, his testament". And so another classic Russian epigram was born (2).

The *Letter* reached Gogol in due course, and he was indeed terribly hurt. Belinskii returned to Russia in September, 1847. Somehow, hundreds and eventually (it was estimated) 20,000 copies of his *Letter* circulated illegally to every Russian of significance, including Nicholas. Presumably both Annenkov and Herzen were primary copyists. Annenkov's lack of fear for Belinskii proved naive. Nicholas's police judged the *Letter* "insolent against the Church" and "politically disappointing", both arrestable offenses, but in the event they held off, because their victim was dying anyway. When Belinskii finally coughed his life away in May, 1848, his *Letter* became a hallowed text, the great man's testament, indeed.

Gogol died relatively young, too, in 1852, desperately

unhappy, having burnt the only copy of his work on the second part of *Dead Souls*, in some ways mad, in some ways serene. Annenkov, a true Russian, was a loyal and even-handed friend to both until the end, and after the end. Thirty years later he wrote in his *Literary Reminiscences*, "The figure of Gogol, afflicted, humble, already pre-pared for anything - the Gogol of his last days - remains my life's most moving recollection, along with the figure of the slowly dying and still restless Belinskii" (4).

During Nicholas's last seven years of intense police terror after the European revolutions of 1848, Belinskii's *Letter* was not a safe document to possess or to have read. In still another famous anecdote, Dostoevskii was arrested and condemned to death in 1849 for (among other heinous crimes) having read the *Letter* aloud to mem-bers of his Petrashevskii circle.

The original sent to Gogol has been lost (by Gogol?) Annenkov's copy given to Herzen was the text that was first pub-lished in his exile journal, the *Polar Star*, in London, in 1855. It could not be published in Russia in a completely uncensored version until after the Revolution of 1905. Lenin somewhat patronizingly described it as "one of the finest works of the uncensored democra-tic press, which has preserved its great and vital importance to this day". Consequently it became a compulsory part of the school curriculum in Communist Russia, where it is regularly described as "an uncompromising attack on feudal and tsarist Russia, an open demand for the end of serfdom and a clarion call for revolution ..." and so on, excessively and endlessly, throughout the Communist world. This has, by reaction, irritated many Westerners into dis-counting Belinskii's *Letter* and his entire career and work.

*　　　　*　　　　*

These political themes do not appear directly in the first page and a half of the *Letter*, which is an introduction on Belinskii's attitude toward Gogol, and, more generally, a statement on how personal relations should be ethically conducted.

Belinskii begins, "You are only partly right in seeing in my article an *angry* man: ..." (5). For this brief half sentence Gogol might have thought Belinskii was writing something conciliatory. "... that word is too weak and inadequate to describe the state I was reduced to when I read your book" (6). Total war has been declared, of course, but initially by heaping guilt on Gogol for hurting Belinskii, who was dying. The personal relationship has not yet been renounced. "But you are completely wrong in ascribing it to your indeed not entirely flattering remarks about the admirers of your talent" (7). (What Belinskii actually wrote was "completely *ne pravy* - not right - to parallel elegantly the "partly *pravy* of the first sentence). Two personal bonds have been snapped in this sentence: Belinskii (though dying) will no longer be a personal object of Gogol's love *or* criticism; he merges himself in a group of critics - and he calls himself and this group

111

admirers of Gogol's impersonal, printed, literary talent, not *a friend* of Gogol the man, as had been so strikingly the case for thirteen years.

"No, there is a more important reason. An outraged sense of self-esteem could be borne, and I would have let the whole thing go by if that were all there was to it. But it is impossible to bear an outraged sense of truth and human dignity. It is impossible to be silent when under the guise of religion and the protection of the knout, lies and unrighteousness are preached as truth and virtue" (8).

The insults here are clear enough: Gogol is unfoundedly insulting Belinskii, who (though dying), is above noticing; he also lies and assaults humanity hypocritically; he doesn't really believe in the Christianity he pretends to; he has made a corrupt deal with Nicholas's police. But one wound is even more painful: Belinskii maintains that a mere personal relation, even an insult, doesn't matter much. It is public positions and politics that are of real ethical importance. No position more contrary to Gogol's vulnerable sense of personal, Christian and Russian decency could be imagined. Belinskii is beginning to address Gogol as if he were a public meeting.

And now, at the beginning of the second paragraph of the *Letter*, there is an apparent abrupt switch back to the personal tie, which is then whisked away in an even stronger assertion of high impersonality: "Yes, I loved you with all the passion with which a man, bound by blood to his country, can honor its hope, honor, glory, one of its great leaders on its path to consciousness, development and progress" (9). This is the rhetoric and cadence with which a Nineteenth Century president of the French Republic decorated a scientist he had never met before. "And you had sound reason to be upset ... when you lost your right to that love. I say that not because I reckon my love an adequate reward for a great talent, but because ... I do not represent one but a multitude of people, most of whom neither you nor I have ever seen ..." (10). There could be no more complete insistence on the triviality of Gogol's cherished, personal, Russian love: I, Belinskii, never did love you as a person: as a multitude we abstractly admired your public achievements!

"I don't know how to give you even the least impression of the indignation your book has stirred up in all noble hearts, or of the wild shouts of joy all your enemies let out when it appeared - both the non-literary (the Chichikovs, the Nozdrevs, the mayors, etc.), [It was particularly mean to select these sleazy scoundrels from Gogol's own greatest works as symbols for his new allies.] and by the literary, whose names you know well .... Even if the book were written out of deep, sincere conviction, it would have had to make the same impression on the public" (11).

This is on the surface another accusation of insincere, pretended religion, but there is a suggestion here of the alternate possibility to which Belinskii will switch back and forth, that Gogol really had turned neurotically to religion. "And if everybody took it as an ingenious but quite ruthless method to achieve

112

n entirely earthly goal by heavenly means - you have no one to blame
ut yourself" (12). This seems even more to suggest that Gogol *was*
sincere and to beseech him through contempt, to draw back from his
new looniness, a return to the personal tie.

This dual message may be sustained in the next passage, more
lacerating to a *writer* than anything that preceded it: "What is surprising is that you find it surprising. I think it is because you
know Russia profoundly only as an artist, not as a thinker, whose
role you have so unsuccessfully tried to take on in your fantastic
book" (13). Does this sentence indicate that Belinskii's careful
balance between the value of the artist and the thinker, discussed
in the last chapter in connection with Goncharov and Herzen, in fact
tipped toward the thinker? Communists have quoted it as if it did
mean that the critic, the philosopher and the ideologue are far
wiser than mere creative writers. But nothing in the grammar forces
an interpretation of imbalance.

So ends Belinskii's introduction to his *Letter*, which sets
forth, as I shall maintain, an important kind of Protestant and
revolutionary view of personal relations: they must be sacrificed,
in a pinch, to larger public ethical concerns of nation and humanity.
And yet the introduction is not without a recurring contrary voice,
a personal plea to friend Gogol to save himself before it is too
late.

In a transitional passage, Belinskii tacks abruptly: "It
isn't that you were not a thinker, but for so many years you have
been looking at Russia from your *beautiful far-away* ...(14) - a
different kind of mean dig at Gogol the voluntary exile, in Rome of
all places with its vile connotations to a Russian. Then Belinskii
tacks again, and resoundingly states the main theme of the *Letter*
the real nature and relation of religion and Russia: "Therefore
you haven't noticed that Russia sees its salvation not in mysticism,
not in asceticism, not in pietism, but in the triumphs of civilization, enlightenment and humanity. She needs not sermons (she has
heard enough of them!), not prayers (she has repeated enough of
them!), but the awakening of the people to a sense of human dignity,
lost for so many centuries in the filth and the garbage, and rights
and laws conforming not to the teachings of the church but to common
sense and justice, and their strictest possible observance" (15).

It is a complex and paradoxical theme expressed in these two
sentences. "Russia *sees*," not "Russia needs" or "we the
intelligentsia see that Russia needs", but the assertion that *all*
Russia, which must include the vast peasantry, already sees through
Orthodox Christianity and wants Western secular progress. The
Russian people may not yet have won human dignity, but it already
sees that the Church is a lie!

This is not the view of Nineteenth Century Russia held in the
modern West, derived essentially from Romantic travelers,
Dostoevskii and Tolstoi. It was not the view of the liberal Russian
writers, Pushkin, Turgenev and Chekhov, who felt varied bittersweet
ambivalences about the immense religiosity of the Russian people
which they only partly deplored, and the secular West in which they
had only partial faith. But it was a major belief of Russian

radicals, as varied as Belinskii, Herzen, Chernyshevskii and Lenin: the tsars, the police and the landlords only pretended to be Christian; the peasant mass of the Russian people was at bottom not fooled, already hated the Church, was already irreligious. Most of Belinskii's *Letter* is on this theme, which, if it were true, would be absolutely central to any analysis of Russia.

Before developing the main theme on Russia and religion, Belinskii fired off his most famous and quoted subversive salvo: "Instead she presents the horrible spectacle of a country where men traffic in men, not having even the excuse so lyingly exploited by American planters, that the Negro is not a man: a country where people don't even have names but only demeaning nicknames: *Vanka, Steshka, Vaska, Palashka:* a country where, finally, there are not only no guarantees of the individual, honor or property, but not even a police order, where there are only huge corporations of different kinds of official thieves and bandits" (16).

When this passage was read aloud in Russia, the hearers often burst out with Russian equivalents of "Right on, Raging Vissarion!". "The most vital, contemporary, national problems in Russia are the annihilation of serfdom, the abolition of corporal punishment and the strictest possible observance of such laws as there are" (17). One must remember that Belinskii's law-and-order stance throughout his *Letter* was not our conservative urge to repress criminals among the poor and the minorities but its opposite, a radical rage against massive bureaucratic corruption and the everyday brutalities of the landlords and the police.

This was indeed a splendid (and risky) rage of Raging Vissarion. It justifies the universal impression that this was an openly revolutionary letter – but this full political blast is not repeated in the remaining 90% of the text. The passage is memorized and quoted around the left world, but it is not the main theme of the *Letter* sent to Gogol on July 3, 1847.

Belinskii shifts his music through several chords from politics back to religion: "And at such a time, a great writer whose own marvelously artistic and profoundly truthful creations contributed so mightily to Russia's self-consciousness, allowing her to look at herself as in a mirror, comes out with a book in which in the name of Christ and the church he teaches the barbarian landlords to grind still more money out of the peasants, to beat their *'unwashed snouts'*! ... Yes, if you had tried to murder me I couldn't hate you more than I do for these revolting lines" (18).

As we read "in the name of Christ and the church", we think this is another accusation that Gogol was a hypocrite, and so it is, for it is followed by, "And after this you want people to believe in the sincerity of your book?" (19). But immediately afterwards we realize that the phrase introduces into the *Letter* a new and important religious idea of Belinskii's, for the very next sentence is: "No, if you had actually been inspired by the truth of Christ and not by the teachings of the devil ... you would have written to the landlord that since his peasants are his brothers in Christ, and since a brother cannot be slave to his brother, he should give them

their freedom ..." (20).

In the introductory part of the *Letter* Belinskii wrote as if he
thought Christianity were deliberately reactionary nonsense foisted
by unbelieving rulers and priests on the masses to keep them quiet,
exactly the sort of thing American student rebels in the 1960s
called "mindfuck". But here and henceforth Belinskii distinguishes
sharply between what he thinks is the false, reactionary nonsense of
the Orthodox Church - and all churches - and the noble, true
Christianity of Christ, conceived of not as a divine being but as a
sterling, human, radical democratic prophet such as Belinskii
himself.

Belinskii's rage continues in the central and crucial passages
of his *Letter:* "Proponent of the knout, apostle of ignorance,
upholder of obscurity and darkness, panegyrist of Tatar morals, what
are you doing? .... That you base such teaching on the orthodox
church, that I can understand; it has always been the supporter of
the knout and the handmaid of despotism; but why have you mixed
Christ in here? What have you found in common between him and any
church, much less the orthodox church? *He* first brought the teaching of liberty, equality and fraternity to the people, and by his
martyrdom placed the seal of truth on that teaching. And this
alone was the *salvation* of the people, until it got organized into a
church and adopted as the basic principle of orthodoxy. But the
church was a hierarchy and therefore an upholder of inequality, the
flatterer of authority and the enemy and persecutor of brotherhood
among men, and has stayed that way until now. But the meaning of
Christ's teaching was revealed by the philosophical movement of the
last century. And that is why someone such as Voltaire, who by
ridicule stamped out the fires of fanaticism and ignorance in
Europe, is of course more the son of Christ, flesh of his flesh and
bone of his bone, than all your priests, bishops, metropolitans and
patriarchs, East and West" (21). And later in the *Letter*, "He who
suffers at the sight of other people's sufferings, who is grieved
when other people are oppressed, he bears Christ in his breast and
doesn't have to make a pilgrimage to Jerusalem" (22).

This was revolutionary heresy to the Orthodox Church, but to
us it seems to be a strangely Christian heresy for a revolutionary.
I believe the resolution of this paradox lies in the recognition of
the *Protestant* aspect of Belinskii and most thoughtful modern revolutionaries. It is an historical commonplace to say that the
Reformation finally triumphed among French intellectuals with the
Enlightenment of the Eighteenth Century. This means that thinking
Frenchmen at the time (and their heirs everywhere) finally assented
to what Protestants had been saying about Catholics for over 200
years: the characteristic Catholic beliefs and rituals are false
and silly, and the Catholic Church as an institution is establishment, oppressive and evil. It is not so widely recognized that
Enlightened Europeans often developed a converse admiration for the
Protestants themselves.

They did not become converted to Protestant theology, alternate Trinitarian beliefs. They selected for admiration many
Protestant views about ethical religion, ethical society and

115

ethical personal behavior, especially the views of socially humble, left Protestant sects. Benjamin Franklin played this to the hilt and it was part of his immense popularity in Paris. The Enlightened gentlemen did not become socially humble Protestants but they often adopted a kind of as-if religious stance: "We are not traditional Christians, but if a person *is*, he should think and act as, say, the Quakers do, and not as the Catholics". Their revolutionary successors at the end of the century and ever since were often persecuted and thrust into positions in which they felt and acted much more like humble and persecuted left Protestants.

What were these left Protestant sentiments so often admired and/or adopted in secular versions by revolutionaries? That inward and spiritual feeling is the essence of any true religion, not externally visible ritual or self-seeking actions. That unvaryingly righteous conduct at a high level, including effective compassion for others, especially the down-trodden, is more important for everyone than the Church thinks. That conduct rather than status or emotional ties makes one eligible for personal friendship and public posts. That many of the things that are terribly wrong with the world can be changed by humans now, without waiting till Judgment Day. That protest and rebellion against these evils is the highest form of compassion and the noblest human activity. That men are in many senses equal and should be treated so in earthly institutions. That the established powers of Church and state are unrighteous and are historical degenerations from earlier, simpler, better arrangements. That Christ's life on earth was his most important role, that he wanted personal righteousness, open defiance of evil, successful resistance with martyrdom for some, and an egalitarian society, all of which he exemplified supremely, while he detested submission to the status quo, divine honors and even any set theological beliefs. Some of this is what has often been called "the Puritanism of revolutionaries".

Insofar as the Russian *intelligentsia* adopted Enlightenment views and sentiments, they adopted this complex, too. They knew about Western Catholics and Protestants, but their emotions centred on the Russian equivalents, the Orthodox Church and the Old Believers. The broad and generous revolutionaries such as Belinskii and Herzen were very much of this temper. Even later revolutionaries such as Marx, Lenin and Mao, in whom dogma-formulating and church-building were so very powerful, had some of this in them.

Belinskii's *Letter to Gogol* begins, as we have seen, with an act dictated by this Protestant-Enlightenment-revolutionary complex: cutting Gogol off from personal friendship because he had lapsed from righteousness. It reaches its first grand orchestral climax by preaching a Christ who is a *complete* fusion of left, low Protestantism and the French Revolution, as opposed to the (Orthodox) Church, always startling to readers who are unaware of this historical continuity. It now goes on to preach another major Protestant-revolutionary complex of beliefs about the nature of religion and the Russian people.

"You really don't know that the clergy is held in common contempt by Russian society and the Russian people? About whom do the

116

Russian people tell dirty stories? About the priest, the priest's wife, the priest's daughter and the priest's servant. Whom do the Russian people term *congenital idiots, heretics, stallions* [i.e. lechers] ? - the priests. Doesn't the priest in Russia represent gluttony, avarice, servility and shamelessness for all Russians? And you don't know all this? Strange? According to you the Russian people is the most religious in the world: a lie! The basis of religion is piety, reverence, fear of God. But the Russian man pronounces the name of God while scratching his backside. He says about the icon, 'If it works, pray to it; if it doesn't work, cover the pots with it'. Look closer and you will see that it is by nature a profoundly atheist people. There is still a lot of superstition in it, but not a bit of religiousness. Superstition dies away with the advance of civilization, but religion often keeps up with it ... The Russian people is different: mystic exaltation just isn't in its nature; it has too much common sense, too clear and positive a mind: perhaps that is the key to its tremendous historical destiny in the future. Religiousness hasn't struck roots even among the clergy, for a few isolated and exclusive personalities distinguished by quiet, cold, ascetic reflectiveness don't prove anything. The majority of the clergy has always been distinguished only for its fat bellies, theological pedantry and savage ignorance. It is wrong to accuse it of intolerance and fanaticism; it might better be praised for an admirable indifference in matters of faith. Religiousness among us appears only in the schismatic sects, so completely contrasting in spirit to the masses, so numerically insignificant" (23).

This section of Belinskii's exposition has an A-B-A form: the Russian clergy are not truly religious - the Russian people are not truly religious - the Russian clergy are not truly religious. But a counterpattern, a-b-b, cuts across this: in the first, 'a' part Belinskii has the people accuse the clergy, while in both 'b' parts he makes statements in his own persona. The 'A' parts accusing the clergy of irreligion and bestial living have many, many parallels in Protestant and revolutionary sermonizing all over the world. But the 'B' section on the Russian people seems at first glance quite un-Protestant and way off the main line of revolutionary thought.

One wonders. Belinskii is employing one of his familiar intellectual tricks, the use of a broad term in a restricted, ideological sense, so as to lead to a paradoxical conclusion. ("Yes, we have no literature". "1847 presented nothing new in literature"). It is not hard to construct his operational definition of "religious" here. The Russian priests are irreligious because they are sunk in eating, money-grubbing, favor-seeking and sex. (The order of their sins - two lists end climactically in sex - is interesting!) True religion is righteous conduct. One cannot be religious if one is a sinner.

The Russian peasant is irreligious because if he can't get what he wants by praying to an icon, he loses faith in its magic power and puts it to plebeian secular use as a pot cover. He is irreligious because he thinks the power is in the board. True religion cannot make use of mediating material objects. The peasant is irreligious because he wants the religious object and the

117

religion to be of petty, earthly use to him. These are, of course, centuries-old Protestant accusations against Catholics. Practically every Protestant Briton and German in the Nineteenth Century thought these things of practically every Italian and Spaniard. That's not religion; that's Catholicism - or Orthodoxy. Religion must be of no earthly self-interest. Religion cannot mean attempts to make God serve us, but our self-abnegation to serve God.

"The Russian man pronounces the name of God while scratching his backside". This has, of course, been the most hilariously famous and quoted of all Belinskii's epigrams, not in writing but orally, especially among the young. It is almost always quoted as the greatest example of his wicked, wonderful blasphemy, but in context it is clearly a passionately religious statement. It is irreligious even to think of God while in a mundane, everyday frame of mind, while performing a normal bodily activity, much less an obscene one. Religion requires a withdrawal from normal, bodily life into a special, unbodily frame of mind, and indeed a special, unbodily disposition of body.

These are all very widespread Protestant sentiments and Puritan beliefs. They do not constitute any formal Protestant definition of religion but they are sentiments which intimately surround it. Revolutionaries believe they are against religion, but if there had to be a religion, that is the kind they think there should have been. They usually have this Protestant attitude toward their own de facto religious ideologies. Lin Piao said people should not recite from Mao's Little Red Book when on the toilet or engaged in sexual intercourse.

All of these views of Belinskii were on one side of an eternal religious controversy. He tried to dispose of the other side's arguments by sovereignly asserting that it had no view, just a grasping fist and a fat belly. But many of the Orthodox *have* been thoughtful, and they have not been so sure the evils of the world will be ended very soon. They do not believe the Kingdom of Heaven is a democracy, and doubt if the Church on earth should be. Many have been as inwardly spiritual and self-abnegating as any Protestant or revolutionary, but they are also brothers of the vast masses who cannot be. They know that communal, external, ritual activity can move many souls toward goodness who are not otherwise easily moved. They know that many sinful priests and some sinful kings have divided souls, not just fat bellies. They feel that if our friend falls into sin, he needs our supportive presence more than our righteous denunciation. They believe that if Christ is anywhere, He was present when Sonia the whore read from the Gospel of St. John to Raskolnikov the murderer.

And if a Russian peasant covered his pots with an icon and pronounced the name of God while scratching his backside, the Orthodox may thank God that Russians - once - assumed the natural every day, local, undangerous presence of God's love, and believed that nothing was so humble, not even a louse bite on the backside, that it ought to be kept apart from God. All this is the other side of the eternal religious controversy.

118

Belinskii was a paradoxical wishful thinker in this passage.
He was disgusted by the Orthodox clergy, non-religious in his sense
and self-indulgent. But the Russian peasantry, equally non-
religious in his sense, but rather superstitious, delighted him.
He can admire true religion, but is very glad the Russians never
attained it, for superstition is easier to slough off than true
religion. If the immense religiosity of the Russian people, noted
by all foreign travelers, was merely superstition, then it would be
easier to enlighten them in order to move Russian society forward,
and easier to move Russian society forward in order to enlighten
them.

*   *   *

This was Belinskii's exposition of his major themes. In the
remaining 60% of his *Letter* he went through developmental variations
and finally a recapitulation. He was skilled at using Ciceronian
devices such as *praeteritia* "I shall not expand upon your dithy-
ramb to the loving bonds between the Russian people and its masters ..." (24) and "I leave it to your conscience to contemplate the
divine beauty of the autocracy (it's safe and, they say, profitable
for you); only continue to contemplate it judiciously from your
beautiful far-away: close up, it's not so beautiful - or safe ..."
(25).

Belinskii seems to flip the pages of Gogol's book back and
forth, recalling items that had infuriated him on first reading. He
probes repeatedly into the most damaging wound - Are you a vile sell-
out or have you gone degradedly mad? - slashing by turns at both
painful possibilities: "With us ... when a man (even a respectable
one) gets the disease well known to psychiatrists under the name
religiosa mania, he immediately burns more incense to the earthly
god than to the heavenly one ..." (26). "Another thing I remember
you saying in your book, which you declared to be a great and incon-
trovertible truth, that to the common people literacy is not only
useless but positively harmful .... May your Byzantine god forgive
you that Byzantine thought ..." (27).

"What seems natural in fools can't seem so in a man of
genius. Some people think your book is the result of mental derange-
ment near to complete madness .... Clearly that book wasn't written
in a day,or a week, or a month, but perhaps in a year or two or
three. There is method in it. Through its careless exposition one
sees premeditation, and the hymn to the powers that be nicely
arranges the earthly affairs of its devout author. That is why one
hears in St. Petersburg that you wrote this book in order to secure
the position of tutor to the son of the heir to the throne ..."(28).
"Your conversion might even be sincere, but ..." (29).

Another developmental variation: your book fails even in its
nefarious intent: "You don't understand the Russian public at all
well. Its character is determined by the condition of Russian
society, in which fresh forces are bubbling and struggling ...

119

Only in literature, in spite of the Tatar censorship, is there life
and forward movement. That is why the title of writer is so honored
among us .... The title of poet, the calling of the literary man
have long since outshone the tinsel of the epaulette and multicolored
uniforms. And that is why universal attention is given to every
liberal tendency, however poor in talent, and why the popularity of
great poets quickly falls when, sincerely or insincerely, they give
themselves to the service of orthodoxy, autocracy and nationality
..." (30). "When the rumor went round that the government wanted to
print many thousands of copies of your book and sell them for a very
low price, my friends were glum, but I told them that in spite of
all that, the book would have no success and would soon be forgotten .... Yes, the Russian has a deep though still undeveloped
instinct for the truth!" (31).

Still another developmental variation: your professed humility makes us sick; Belinskii was revolted by Gogol's rejection of
his own earlier works, especially *Dead Souls*, and detected a false
pride in this allegedly humble self-deprecation, as thirty five
years later Turgenev would be saddened when Tolstoi renounced his
own works with an even stranger mixture of humility and pride.
Belinskii roared at Gogol's humility in general: "The humility you
preach is first of all not new, and secondly it seems on the one hand
like frightful pride and on the other like the most shameful abase-
ment of your human dignity. Your idea of becoming an abstract perfection, of becoming highest of all in humility, is the result either
of pride or of weakmindedness, and in either case leads inevitably
to hypocrisy, sanctimoniousness and Chinaism .... This is vile, for
if a man who strikes his neighbor on the cheek arouses anger, a man
who strikes himself on the cheek inspires contempt. No! You are
befogged, not illuminated; you don't understand either the spirit
or the form of the Christianity of our time. Your book exudes not
true Christian teaching but the sick fear of death, the devil and
hell" (32).

Final and in some ways most lacerating developmental variation: you are a writer, but now you don't write well any more: "And
what language, what phrases! *'Filth and a rag is now each man'*. Do
you really think that to say *vsiak* [the archaic form of *each*] instead
of *vsiakii* [the modern form of *each*] makes it Biblical? How
exceedingly true it is that when a man gives himself up to lies,
brain and talent desert him. If your book didn't carry your name ...
who would think this turgid and disgusting tinsel of words and phrases was the product of the pen of the author of *The Inspector-
General* and *Dead Souls?*" (33).

The final two pages of recapitulation summarize the introductory section of the *Letter* on the relations between Belinskii and
Gogol rather than the main exposition and development on religion
and Russia. This technique allows Belinskii to conclude with a
grand orchestral climax which both booms his high public truth and
magisterially - yet with a strong personal note again - exhorts
Gogol to repent, to return to his true *métier* as a great creative
writer, and thus to make the resumption of their old friendship
possible. "The unexpected receipt of your letter gave me the chance
to unload on you everything which had piled up in my soul against

you because of your book. I can't speak by halves, I can't be crafty; it's not my nature .... It's not a question of my personality or yours; it is a matter of much greater importance than I am, or even you; it is an issue of truth, of Russian society, of Russia. And here is my last, concluding word: if you have had the misfortune to disown, in proud humility, your truly great works, now disown, with sincere humility, your last book, and atone for the deadly sin of its publication with new creations which will remind us of your former ones" (34).

If a small part of this *Letter* openly trumpets Belinskii's revolutionary aims toward human freedom and dignity, the larger part expounds his deepest, secularly religious convictions about how a man of freedom and dignity, how a revolutionary should feel, act and *be*. I believe this confirms Herzen's initial and instinctively correct insight: Belinskii's *Letter to Gogol* is his testament.

CHAPTER 10

CONCLUSION

READING Belinskii is like reading the Russian realist novels
he inspired. Like them, he grabs us by the lapel, harrows us not so
much by his arguments as by the vehemence and agony of his whole
being, challenges our most basic values and feelings, and demands
that we change our whole lives. We recover ourselves, but are not
entirely certain that we should have. This existential quality of
the man and of the nation that made him *must* be reflected in any
reading of or writing on Belinskii. Most of what he said is simply
part of the past, but then, as in the Russian novels, he comes to a
question that still consumes us, or should. It is not like the
study of Pharaonic ritual texts or the classification of Nematode
worms. We have to figure out our responses to his passionate
challenges, and what is associated with them, and their moral consequences in our own cultural, political and private lives. How *do*
we judge politics in the novel? At this late date, can we be either
for or against the revolution? How do *we* respond to a friend who
has sinned?

A book on Belinskii that does not take him with moral seriousness, that does not at least explain how some of our quandaries are
descended from and parallel to some of his, is not only un-Russian
and inhuman, it is inappropriate. A book on Belinskii has to resist
being wholly caught up in the spirit of Belinskii – for reasons of
modern scholarly and social decorum – but it must *partly* allow
itself to be captured by him. I have tried to write such a book.

An account of Belinskii's life tells us much about his incan-
descent nature. The great memoirists take us right into the flame.
A survey of his philosophical and critical position prepares us for
the heat but is of itself cold. Only by reading his works themselves can we catch fire. To read him as he wrote his essays is
extraordinarily different from summarizing his thought. Suddenly a
worthy but obsolete Romantic, an historical monument, becomes a
living human being in the room with us. We come to know his minor
thoughts as well as his major theses, his ways of approaching, back-
ing and filling, and avoiding, his loves, peeves and inconsistencies, the language of his thundering sermonizing and the pace of his
wit, the books he read and the abstract nouns that moved him, what a
person is like who lives fearlessly and how it is to die for years
on end. We become sure we know what *he* was like, what made him

tick, how he would respond to a given stimulus, what he would do
next.

Or do we know it? Belinskii in his letters left us a number
of charming statements about how he was all in a muddle when he
wrote, about how his most successful pieces came when he sat down
and started writing with no idea of where he would go. He has convinced those who read these statements, and yet if one reads those
successful works with an eye to structure, structures emerge, so
detailed and effective that it defies belief that they just poured
out by rambling chance. Neither side of this paradox about Belinskii,
or of a number of other paradoxes, can be wholly discounted. We *can*
penetrate to the core of Belinskii and in that core there are
several mysteries.

Belinskii was one of the most convincing, effective, opinion-
marshaling writers who ever lived. To begin with, much of it was
because he preached ideas whose time had come. Late in life he convinced because he was the great Belinskii, and after his death
because he was that and a moving martyr as well. But in between
these factors, both chronologically and psychologically, he convinced because he *wrote* convincingly. That should not have happened;
people should respond to soundness of thought, not effectiveness of
presentation. But it did happen. A book on Belinskii should dwell
on the techniques and flavor of his writing - conscious or
unconscious - as well as its content, not only to grasp Belinskii
himself, but to comprehend his effectiveness which *was* his historical importance. I have tried to write such a book.

Belinskii died in May, 1848, but he is one of the revolutionary heroes of whom the Communists say, "He lives forever in the
hearts of the people". The afterlife of this immortal has been
somewhat complicated. Immediately after his death came the last
Seven Mad Years of Nicholas I's reign, by all odds the worst period
of police terror in Russia until the Communists seized power.
During this period Belinskii was an unperson. His name, principles
and works could not be printed, mentioned publicly, quoted or
referred to. The *Letter to Gogol* was the cause or excuse for sending a number of people to Siberia along with Dostoevskii. Belinskii
was remembered, of course, as a wonderful and tragic figure whose
death had marked the plunging of Russia from Nekrasov's green spring
back into Nicholas's winter.

Then the great tyrant died, discredited by the loss of the
Crimean War, in 1855, and his son, Alexander II, ended the police
frenzy, began an eleven year period of "Great Reforms" including the
emancipation of the serfs, and brought back the spring. Belinskii's
works and memory were not completely freed from censorship, but radical journalists used his tried and true techniques to convey anything they really wanted to say about Belinskii.

For the first seven years of the new reign, Russia had a new
literary dictator, a self-conscious successor to Belinskii. This
was Nikolai Chernyshevskii (1828-1889), another *raznochinets* from
the Volga area, another writer for and editor of the *Contemporary*
along with Nakrasov, another sovereign literary critic who made and

broke reputations, another discoverer of new talent who hailed
Tolstoi, a much more open and explicit political revolutionary by no
means satisfied with the mere emancipation of the serfs, another
admitted leader of the *intelligentsia* and now the revolutionary movement of his day. Not having tuberculosis, he was arrested in 1862
and sent to Siberia for over twenty years.

Chernyshevskii's most ambitious effort at literary criticism
was a book length study, *Essays on the Gogol Period of Russian
Literature,* which appeared in the *Contemporary* in 1855 and 1856.
Following Belinskii's pattern, Chernyshevskii freely took off from
the subject at hand, in this case Gogol, to his real subject,
Belinskii and revolutionary exhortation. Belinskii's achievements
were detailed and praised as much as was possible during that thaw
in the censorship, and doubly praised by being so strikingly imita-
ted. Chernyshevskii was a less vulnerable and heart-warming person
and mind than Belinskii, but his admiration for his predecessor was
unstinting. These essays formally canonized Belinskii's place in
Russian history for the *intelligentsia,* as Belinskii had once canonized Pushkin.

When Chernyshevskii was struck down and Alexander II relapsed
into a milder version of the repressions of his father, the revolutionaries grew more numerous, extreme, divided and sectarian. In
this period, 1866–1881, Belinskii's reputation evolved into what it
has been for most people who have heard of him ever since. He was
a founding hero of the movement, but by now a dead grandfather.
His life and personality became a great, tragic, national memory.
This was the period when his friends, in late middle age, brought
out the great memoirs of Belinskii which have made his personality
so memorable in literature. He was now seen as a glorious and for-
tunate early leader of the movement when it was still united. He
never lived to have to make the detailed decisions on ideology,
stance and tactics which were splitting the Russian revolutionaries
hopelessly in the 1870s. All could look back at him for generalized
inspiration, with admiration and envy. Besides, hadn't he been a
nicer person than Chernyshevskii, to say nothing of the
terrorists?

There were dissenters from this consensus of the dissenters.
Conservatives still disagreed with him, but their wrath had more
recent objects. Dostoevskii, now Christian, Slavophile and conservative, had very mixed memories of Belinskii, and his memoirs of
his first patron were indeed violently mixed. The critic Apollon
Grigoriev (1812–1864) regarded himself as a conservative disciple
of Belinskii, and thought him a seminal figure in the 1830s who had
taken a wrong left turn toward the wrong kind of social realism in
the 1840s.

But the abiding pattern of disesteem of Belinskii emerged
only in the next, Silver Age of Russian culture, ca. 1890–1917. By
this time the great period of realist novels had receded all over
Europe and therefore Russians, too, moved on to new waves of the
future. The Russian revolutionary movement was thoroughly crushed
and kept from being reborn for most of the reign of Alexander III
(1881–1894). The cultural fire of the new generation was incredibly
rich, diverse and resistant to classification, but we call it the

Symbolist movement, which ranged from the philosophy of Soloviev through the poems of Blok and the paintings of Vrubel' to the ballets of Diaghilev. What the Symbolists reacted against and disliked is much easier to delimit.

The Symbolists admired the great realist novels but thought that age was over, preferring shorter forms and more colorful, sensuous, allusive, religious, erotic and neurotic themes and atmospheres. They were mostly detached liberals or apolitical and had no faith in the reviving revolutionary movement of the 1890s. What they couldn't stand was crude politicking in literature of any art, any social-political dictation to culture. The greatests realists were above that, but the Symbolists knew all the second and third rate and trashy tendentious left writing of that Russian generation, too, and fought the good and successful fight to free Russian culture (for a generation) from it.

This left them with a mixed attitude toward Belinskii. He was granted to have been a wonderful person, and to have struggled nobly to free Russian from the darkness of Nicholas I and his times. But he was judged an early and fairly unsophisticated literary mind, who with the best of intentions began a baleful fifty years of left, message-laden pressure on Russian literature, which drowned all save the Himalayan peaks, and still remained to be fought at every turn. Belinskii's misguided literary aims were reflected in his own miserable writing. Blok went so far as to say that Belinskii did more damage to Russian literature than the censors, for they postponed publications, but Belinskii poisoned its sources, the writers themselves. Until 1917 the Symbolists believed that they were winning the battle and forcing Belinskian realism into the past, so they couldn't hate him.

These two developed positions on Belinskii are still with us. The revived revolutionaries after 1895 by and large ignored Symbolist Russian culture and maintained the Belinskii-Chernyshevskii position. The Communists were always strongly for their rather narrow conception of the Belinskian tradition and for tendentious realism, but this became the one, total dogma of the land only after Stalin closed in at the end of the 1920s. Belinskii has been a compulsory cultural and political hero in Communist Russia ever since. This made him the beneficiary of a great deal of meticulous if unimaginitive scholarship and of wide and complete publication. His texts are available for anyone who may in the future want to use them, subversively, to promote human freedom and dignity in Russia.

The Symbolists and their linear successors in Russia, the early Twentieth Century Modernists of many schools, survived until Stalin. Since then the few who escaped into exile have inevitably allowed their horror at Stalin's inconceivably murderous tyranny and at his totalitarian methods of enforcing the travesty of Nineteenth Century realism which he called "socialist realism", to project backwards. It was a much more terrible charge that was laid at Belinskii's door after 1930: he was grandiloquently honored by *that* régime, he was an important ancestor of *that* cultural monstrosity.

Belinskii was not really known outside of Russia in the

Nineteenth Century, although his inspirations, the Russian novel and the Russian revolutionary movement, became world famous. The first serious work on Russian thought by a foreigner appeared in German in 1913. This was *The Spirit of Russia* by Thomas Masaryk, a philosopher soon to become the founder of Czechoslovakia. He favored Belinskii as a person and as a political and literary influence, but criticized him philosophically from Masaryk's own Kantian point of view. After the First World War a wave of Russian exiles discussed Belinskii in their studies of Russia, usually liking the man, deploring his style, noting his role in promoting realism and lamenting his ultimate inspiration of the Communists. Only in Japan did Belinskii, along with Gogol, enjoy extensive translation and wide critical influence on the new westernizing leftists of the early Twentieth Century and the new westernizing writers – a strange partial duplication of his original influence in Russia.

After World War II the tremendous burst of Cold War scholarship in Western countries on Russia produced few translations but many intellectual studies of Belinskii and a few full-length books. The early shorter studies were rather unfavorable; the horror at the then living Stalin was too great. Later estimates as the Cold War receded into the past, whether by liberal scholars or by Marxists seeking to transcend Stalin's heritage have been much more favorable: Belinskii was a noble soul – and a dear. His thought was German, abstract and naive, but his ability to make literary discoveries was astonishing. His intended influence on literature was more balanced than his successors made it out to be. Although a wretched writer, he was in general an attractive figure in comparison with the more adamant Generation of the 1860s, and he cannot be blamed for Stalin's atrocities in his name a hundred years later – though there *is* a continuity of some ideas and attitudes.

This last paragraph, I think, briefly describes the present consensus of the relatively few Westerners, mostly Russianists, comparative literature scholars and intellectual radicals, who have heard of Belinskii. What if *this* little book should have some influence?

There is no need to repeat the many glowing things I have said about Belinskii's life and personality, his ability to inspire, discover and be described by great Russian realist writers, his doughty fight against the evils that crushed Russia and his inspiration of the later revolutionaries who carried on that fight. He *was* a wonderful person, a good person and a great historical force. The abiding questions are about the quality of his mind and soul. I think he was a much better writer than most people do, but he was not a Turgenev. His mind and sensibility were broader, more complex and contradictory, more defensible today than any brief discussion of him can indicate, but did he really measure up to our highest standards for a Nineteenth Century mind? – a Tolstoi or a George Eliot?

The answer has to be, no. I admire Belinskii's mind a great deal, but I love him more than I admire him. I unquestioningly look up to the minds of Turgenev and Tolstoi, Mill and Eliot, but I have to confess to looking down a bit at Belinskii's, to

indulging him. Our scholarly and literary worlds will agree,
brusquely or sadly.

But I cannot be certain of this judgment. I have no fear
that I praise Belinskii too highly, unusually high as my praise is
these days in the West. It is Herzen, Turgenev and Tolstoi whom I
fear. They really respected Belinskii's mind significantly more
than I do. And they also knew him, even Tolstoi who had never met
him personally, as I never can. My mind, after much study, rates
Belinskii high, but not with the highest. But the great minds who
knew him recognized him as a peer, and I cannot say that I know
they were mistaken. This is the ultimate question in judging
Belinskii, and who has the arrogance to say the question is not
still open?

NOTES AND REFERENCES

CHAPTER 1

1. D.S. Mirsky, *A History of Russian Literature* (New York; Alfred Knopf, 1949), pp. 167-68.

CHAPTER 2

1. A.I. Gertsen (A.I. Herzen), *Sobranie sochinenii (Collected Works)*, Tom IX (Volume IX) (Moscow: Izdatel'stvo Akademii Nauk SSSR, 1956) pp. 35-36.

CHAPTER 3

1. I.S. Turgenev, *Sochineniia (Works)*, Tom 14 (Volume 14) (Moscow-Leningrad: Izdatel'stvo "Nauka", 1967), pp. 24-26.

2. Ibid., p. 27.

3. Ibid., p. 30.

4. Ibid., p. 31.

5. Ibid., p. 53.

6. Loc. cit.

7. Ibid., p. 44.

8. Ibid., p. 46.

9. Ibid., p. 45.

10. Ibid., p. 32.

11. Ibid., p. 45-46.

12. Ibid., pp. 28-29.

13. Ibid., p. 55.

14. Ibid., p. 62.

15. A.I. Herzen, *Sobranie sochinenii*, Tom IX, p. 28.

16. Ibid., pp. 28-29.

17. Ibid., p. 29.

18. Ibid., pp. 30-32.

19. Ibid., p. 32.

20. Ibid., pp. 33-34.

21. Ibid., p. 34.

22. P.V. Annenkov, *Literaturnye vospominaniia (Literary Reminiscences)* (Moscow: Gosudarstvennoe izdatel'stvo khudozhestvennoi literatury, 1960), pp. 146-47.

23. Ibid., pp. 172-73.

24. Ibid., p. 234.

25. Ibid., 236-37.

26. Ibid., p. 282.

27. Ibid., p. 333.

28. Ibid., p. 346.

29. Ibid., p. 368.

CHAPTER 5

1. Herbert Bowman, *Vissarion Belinski, 1811-1848; A Study in the Origins of Social Criticism in Russia* (Cambridge: Harvard University Press, 1954), pp. 54-66.

2. Author's class notes for a lecture by Geroid Tanquary Robinson, in his course, *The History of Russian Social Thought*, at Columbia University, spring term, 1953.

3. V.G. Belinskii, *Polnoe sobranie sochinenii (Complete Collected Works)* (Moscow: Izdatel'stvo Akademii Nauk SSSR, 1953-1956), Tom I (Volume I), p. 20.

4. Loc. cit.

5. Loc. cit.

6. Ibid., pp. 21-22.

7. Ibid., p. 22.

8. Ibid., p. 23.

9. Ibid., p. 24.

10. Ibid., pp. 28-29.

11. Ibid., p. 30.

12. Loc. cit.

13. Loc. cit.

14. Ibid., p. 32.

15. Loc. cit.

16. Ibid., p. 33.

17. Ibid., p. 34.

18. Loc. cit.

19. Ibid., p. 35.

20. Loc. cit.

21. Ibid., pp. 35-36.

22. Ibid., p. 36.

23. Ibid., p. 37.

24. Ibid.,p. 38.

25. Loc. cit.

26. Ibid., p. 39.

27. Ibid., p. 42.

28. Ibid., p. 65n.

29. Ibid., p. 45.

30. Ibid., p. 53.

31 Ibid., pp. 67-68

32. Ibid., p. 69.

33. Ibid., p. 68.

34. Ibid., p. 69.

35. Ibid., pp. 69-70.

36. Ibid., p. 86.

37. Ibid., p. 87.

38. Ibid., p. 89.

39. Ibid., p. 97.

40. Ibid., p. 94.

41. Ibid., p. 102.

42. Ibid., p. 103.

43. Loc. cit.

44. Ibit., p. 104.

CHAPTER   6

1. V.G. Belinskii, *Polnoe sobranie sochinenii*, Tom VII, p. 100.

2. Ibid., pp. 431-32.

3. Ibid., p. 432.

4. Loc. cit.

5. Ibid., p. 435.

6. Ibid., p. 438.

7. Ibid., p. 439.

8. Loc. cit.

9. Ibid., p. 436.

10. Ibid., p. 440.

11. Loc. cit.

12. Ibid., p. 452.

13. Ibid., p. 453.

14. Ibid., p. 454.

15. Loc. cit.

16. Ibid., p. 457.

17. Ibid., p. 458.

18. Loc. cit.

19. Loc. cit.

20. Ibid., p. 460.

21. Ibid., p. 466.

22. Ibid., p. 467.

23. Ibid., p. 469.

24. Ibid., p. 470.

25. Ibid., p. 471.

26. Ibid., p. 472.

27. Ibid., p. 473.

28. Loc. cit.

29. Loc. cit.

30. Ibid., pp. 475-76.

31. Ibid., p. 475.

32. Ibid., pp. 476-77.

33. Ibid., pp. 477-78.

34. Ibid., p. 480.

35. Loc. cit.

36. Ibid., p. 482.

37. Ibid., p. 483.

38. Loc. cit.

39. Ibid., p. 484, a paraphrase of *Revelations* 3: 14-16.

40. Ibid., pp. 484-85.

41. Ibid., p. 491.

42. Ibid., p. 501.

43. Loc. cit.

44. Loc. cit.

45. Ibid., p. 502.

46. Ibid., p. 509.

CHAPTER 7

1. V.G. Belinskii, *Polnoe sobranie sochinenii*, Tom X, p. 7.

2. Loc. cit.

3. Loc. cit.

4. Ibid., p. 9.

5. Loc. cit.

6. Ibid., p. 14.

7. Ibid., p. 17.

8. Loc. cit.

9. Loc. cit.

10. Loc. cit.

11. Loc. cit.

12. Loc. cit.

13. Loc. cit.

14. Ibid., pp. 17-18.

15. Ibid., p. 18.

16. Loc. cit.

17. Ibid., p. 19.

18. Ibid., p. 23.

19. Loc. cit.

20. Ibid., p. 24.

21. Ibid., pp. 26-27.

22. Ibid., p. 27.

23. Ibid., p. 28.

24. Ibid., pp. 28-29.

25. Ibid., p. 29.

26. Ibid., p. 30.

27. Ibid., p. 32.

28. Loc. cit.

29. Ibid., p. 33.

30. Loc. cit.

31. Ibid., pp. 39-40.

32. Ibid., p. 40.

33. Loc. cit.

34. Loc. cit.

35. Loc. cit.

36. Loc. cit.

37. Ibid., p. 41.

38. Loc. cit.

39. Loc. cit.

CHAPTER 8

1. V.G. Belinskii, *Polnoe sobranie sochinenii*, Tom X, p. 355.

2. Ibid., p. 279.

3. Ibid., p. 280.

4. Ibid., p. 287.

5. Loc. cit.

6. Ibid., p. 293.

7. Ibid., p. 294.

8. Loc. cit.

9. Ibid., p. 296.

10. Ibid., pp. 307-08.

11. Ibid., p. 308.

12. Loc. cit.

13. Loc. cit.

14. P.V. Annenkov, *Literaturnye vospominaniia*, p. 366.

15. Loc. cit.

16. Belinskii, op. cit., Tom XII, p. 384.

17. Loc. cit.

18. Ibid., Tom X, p. 308.

19. Loc. cit.

20. Loc. cit.

21. Loc. cit.

22. Ibid., pp. 308-09.

23. Ibid., p. 309.

24. Ibid., p. 314.

25. Ibid., p. 315.

26. Ibid., p. 317.

27. Ibid., p. 320.

28. Ibid., p. 318.

29. Ibid., p. 323.

30. Ibid., p. 326.

31. Ibid., p. 344.

32. Loc. cit.

33. Ibid., p. 345.

34. Ibid., p. 346.

35. Ibid., p. 351.

36. Ibid., p. 358.

CHAPTER 9

1. V.G. Belinskii, *Polnoe sobranie sochinenii*, Tom XII, p. 356.

2. N.V. Gogol', *Polnoe sobranie sochinenii (Complete Collected Works)*, Tom XIII (Volume XII) (Moscow: Izdatel'stvo Akademii Nauk SSSR, 1952), pp. 326-28.

3. P.V. Annenkov, *Literaturnye vospominaniia*, pp. 361-63.

4. Ibid., p. 212.

5. Belinskii, op. cit., Tom X, p. 212.

6. Loc. cit.

7. Loc. cit.

8. Loc. cit.

9. Loc. cit.

10. Loc. cit.

11. Loc. cit.

12. Ibid., pp. 212-13.

13. Ibid., p. 213.

14. Loc. cit.

15. Loc. cit.

16. Loc. cit.

17. Loc. cit.

18. Ibid., pp. 213-14.

19. Ibid., p. 214.

20. Loc. cit.

21. Ibid., pp. 214-15.

22. Ibid., p. 218.

23. Ibid., p. 215.

24. Loc. cit.

25. Ibid., p. 216.

26. Loc. cit.

27. Loc. cit.

28. Ibid., pp. 216-17.

29. Ibid., p. 218.

30. Ibid., p. 217.

31. Ibid., p. 218.

32. Loc. cit.

33. Ibid., pp. 218-19.

34 Ibid., p. 220.

SELECTED BIBLIOGRAPHY

PRIMARY SOURCES

WORKS BY BELINSKII IN RUSSIAN

Sochineniia V. Belinskogo (Collected Works of V. Belinskii), 2nd
Edition, 12 volumes. Moscow: Izdatel'stvo K. Soldatenkova i
N. Shchepkina, 1860-1865. This is the earliest edition, incom-
plete and partly censored, available in any American library.

Sobranie sochinenii (Collected Works), Jubilee Edition, 3 volumes.
St. Petersburg: Biblioteka russkikh kritikov, 1911. This
edition, edited by the famous populist critic, Ivanov-Razumnik,
was the finest published under the tsarist régime.

Polnoe sobranie sochinenii (Complete Collected Works), 13 volumes.
Moscow: Akademiia nauk SSSR, Institut russkoi literatury, 1953-
1956. This is the standard Soviet edition, complete with
variorum material and facsimiles of a number of Belinskii's
manuscript sheets, Stalinist in commentary. Since this there
have been several selected editions, chiefly of Belinskii's
writings on Pushkin, Lermontov and Gogol, published in Moscow
in the 1960s and 1970s.

TRANSLATIONS OF WORKS BY BELINSKII

Belinsky, V.G., *Selected Philosophical Works*. Moscow: Foreign
Languages Publishing House, 1948, reprinted 1956. This is a
large (552 pp.) selection of the most important works and
letters of Belinskii, including all of those analyzed at length
in this book. Its commentary is Stalinist and its accurate
but unexciting translations have been the basis of virtually
all other versions of works of Belinskii to appear in English.

Edie, James M., Scanlan, James P., Zeldin, Mary-Barbara, editors,
with the collaboration of George L. Kline, *Russian Philosophy*,
Volume I. Chicago: Quadrangle Books, 1965. A smaller selection, better translated, with sophisticated commentary by
knowledgeable philosophers.

Matlaw, Ralph E., editor, *Belinsky, Chernyshevsky and Dobrolyubov*. New York: E.P. Dutton, 1962. Another smaller selection, better translated, with an intelligent introduction.

The Letter to Gogol has appeared in a number of anthologies of Russian documents. It is perhaps most easily available in Riha, Thomas, ed. *Readings in Russian Civilization*, Volume II, Chicago: University of Chicago Press, 1964 and several later editions.

SECONDARY SOURCES

HISTORIES

Florinsky, Michael T., *Russia, A History and an Interpretation*, Volume II. New York: The Macmillan Company, 1955. This is the standard work in English on Russian history in the last century of the tsarist régime.

Lincoln, W. Bruce, *Nicholas I*. Bloomington: Indiana University Press, 1978. Now the definitive biography in English.

MEMOIRS

Annenkov, P.V., *Literaturnye vospominaniia (Literary Reminiscences)*. Moscow: Gosudarstvennoe izdatel'stvo khudozhestvennoi literatury, 1960. Translated by Irwin R. Titunik as *The Extraordinary Decade: Literary Memoirs by P.V. Annenkov*, edited by Arthur Mendel. Ann Arbor: University of Michigan Press, 1968.

Gertsen, A.I., (A.I. Herzen), *Sobranie sochinenii (Collected Works)*, Volume IX. Moscow: Izdatel'stvo Akademii nauk SSSR, 1956. This volume contains the standard Russian text and comment on the second part of Herzen's memoirs, which describe Belinskii. Translated by Constance Garnett as *My Past and Thoughts: the Memoirs of Alexander Herzen*, Volume 2. New York: Alfred Knopf, 1968.

Turgenev, I.S., *Sochineniia (Works)*, Volume 14. Moscow-Leningrad: Izdatel'stvo "Nauk," 1967. This is the standard Russian text of Turgenev's literary memoirs. Translated by David Magarshack as *Literary Reminiscences and Autobiographical Fragments*. New York: Farrar, Straus & Cudahy, 1958.

STUDIES OF BELINSKII IN ENGLISH

Berlin, Isaiah, Sir, *Russian Thinkers*, edited by Henry Hardy and Aileen Kelly. London: Hogarth Press, 1978. This collection of essays contains the brilliant *The Marvelous Decade, 1838-1848*.

Bowman, Herbert E., *Vissarion Belinski (1811-1848); a Study in the Origins of Social Criticism in Russia*. Cambridge: Harvard University Press, 1954. This, the first full length monograph on Belinskii in English, and the only one for twenty years, has well served a whole generation of Russianists.

Brown, Edward James, *Stankevich and His Moscow Circle, 1830-1840*. Stanford: Stanford University Press, 1966.

Dolenc, Ivan, *Dostoevskii and Christ: a Study of Dostoevskii's Rebellion Against Belinskii*. Toronto and New York: Publishing and Print Co., 1978.

Frank, Joseph, *Dostoevsky: the Seeds of Revolt, 1821-1849*. Princeton: Princeton University Press, 1976. A most impressive and well-received work.

Lampert, Evgenii, *Studies in Rebellion*. London: Routledge and Kegan Paul, 1957.

Hare, Richard, *Pioneers of Russian Social Thought*. London and New York: Oxford University Press, 1951.

Lossky, N.O., *History of Russian Philosophy*, Volume I. New York: International Universities Press, 1951. By an exiled Russian Orthodox philosopher.

Masaryk, Thomas Garrigue, *The Spirit of Russia*, Volume I. London: George Allen and Unwin, and New York: The Macmillan Company, 1919. The first professional study of Russian thought in its original German and in English, by a Kantian philosopher who later became the founder and first president of Czechoslovakia.

Mathewson, Rufus, Jr., *The Positive Hero in Russian Literature*, New York: Columbia University Press, 1958.

Proctor, Thelwall, *Dostoevskij and the Belinskij School of Literary Criticism*. The Hague: Mouton, 1969.

Smirnov, Z.V., *The Socio-Political and Philosophical Views of V.G. Belinsky*. Moscow: Foreign Languages Publishing House, 1955. A translation of a widely used Soviet pamphlet.

Terras,Victor, *Belinsky and Russian Literary Criticism: the Heritage of Organic Aesthetics*. Madison: University of Wisconsin Press, 1974. A most sophisticated contemporary work

on the subject, the second full length monograph on
Belinskii in English.

Tompkins, Stuart Ramsey, *The Russian Intelligentsia; the Making of
the Revolutionary State.* Norman: University of Oklahoma
Press, 1957.

Yarmolinsky, Avrahm, *Road to Revolution.* New York: Collier Books,
1962.

Zenkovsky, V.V., *A History of Russian Philosophy,* translated by
George L. Kline, Volume I. New York: Columbia University
Press, 1953. By an exiled Russian philosopher and priest.

STUDIES OF BELINSKII IN RUSSIAN

There is an enormous literature on Belinskii in Russian, most
of the first hundred years of which is not available in any
American library. It might be useful to list some of the recent,
post-Stalin works published in the U.S.S.R. which have found their
way to America, and a few older books as well.

Akademii nauk SSSR: Institut mirovoi literatury, *Belinskii i
sovremennost' (Belinskii and the Present Time),* edited by
D.D. Blagoi and others. Moscow, 1964.

Bel'chikov, Iu.A., *Obshchestvenno-politicheskaia leksika V.G.
Belinskogo (A Social-Political Dictionary of V.G. Belinskii).*
Moscow: Izdatel'stvo Moskovskogo universiteta, 1962.

Berezina, V.G., *Belinskii i voprosy istorii russkoi zhurnalistiki
(Belinskii and Questions of the History of Russian Journalism).*
Leningrad: Izdatel'stvo Leningradskogo universiteta, 1973.

Fedorov, M.G., *Russkaia progressivnaia mysl' XIX v.: ot geografi-
cheskkogo determinizma k istoricheskomu materializme (Russian
Progressive Thought in the Nineteenth Century; From
Geographical Determinism to Historical Materialism).*
Novosibirsk: Akademii nauk SSSR, 1972. An unideological study
of this transition, willing to recognize how un-Marxist
Belinskii's geographical and national determinism was.

Filatova, E.M., *Belinskii.* Moscow: "Mysl'". 1976. A short,
popular work.

Guliaev, N.A., *Nekotorye voprosy teorii iskusstvu v sochineniiakh
V.G. Belinskogo (Several Questions of artistic theory in the
Works of V.G. Belinskii).* Tomsk: Tomskii gosudarstvennyi
universitet, 1957.

_____, *V.G. Belinskii i zarubezhnaia estetika ego vremeni (V.G. Belinskii and the Foreign Aesthetic of His Time)*, Kazan: Izdatel'stvo Kazanskogo universiteta, 1961. Unusually willing, for a Soviet author, to admit foreign influence on Belinskii.

Ivanov-Razumnik (pseudonym), *Velikaia iskaniia (The Great Searchings)*. St. Petersburg: Prometei, 1912.

Katrich, V.M., *Kritika kapitalisticheskogo stroia i burzhuaznogo gosudarstva V.G. Belinskim i A.I. Gertsenom (Criticism of the Capitalist System and the Bourgeois State in V.G. Belinskii and A.I. Herzen)*. Kiev: Izdatel'stvo Kievskogo universiteta, 1960. An orthodox Communist work.

Kirpotin, V.Ia., *Dostoevskii i Belinskii (Dostoevskii and Belinskii)*. Moscow: Khudozhestvennaia literatura, 1976. An unideological work, fair to both writers.

Lavretskii, A., *Belinskii, Chernyshevskii, Dobroliubov v bor'be za realizm (Belinskii, Chernyshevskii, Dobroliubov in the struggle for Realism)*. Moscow: Khudozhestvennaia literatura, 1968.

_____, *Estetika Belinskogo (The Aesthetics of Belinskii)*. Moscow: Akademiia nauk, Institut morovoi literatury, 1959.

Mezentsev, D.A., *Belinskii: problema ideinogo razvitiia i tvorcheskogo naslediia (Belinskii and the Problem of Ideal Development and the Creative Heritage)*. Moscow: Sovetskii pisatel', 1957.

_____, *Belinskii i russkaia literatura (Belinskii and Russian Literature)*. Moscow: Prosveshchenie, 1965.

Nechaeva, V.S., *V.G. Belinskii*, 4 volumes. Moscow: Akademiia nauk SSSR, 1949-1967. The heaviest work of Soviet scholarship on Belinskii, begun under Stalin and not varying much from his principles.

Oksman, Iu.G., *Letopis' zhizni i tvorchestva V.G. Belinskogo (A Chronicle of the Life and Creative Works of V.G. Belinskii)*. Moscow: Gosudarstvennoe izdatel'stvo khudozhestvennoi literatury, 1958. A useful example of a valuable genre of Soviet scholarship, the chronicle of all known doings and writings of a noted figure, day by day as much as possible.

Panov, D.A., *Lingvisticheskie vzgliady V.G. Belinskogo (The Linguistic Views of V.G. Belinskii)*. Saratov: Saratovskoe knizhnoe izdatel'stvo, 1959.

Pekhtelev, I.G., *Belinskii -- istorik russkoi literatury (Belinskii -- Historian of Russina Literature)*. Moscow: Gosudarstvennoe uchebno-pedagogicheskoe izdatel'stvo, 1961. A high school text.

Piksanov, N.K. and others, *Letopis' zhizni Belinskogo (A Chronicle of the Life of Belinskii)*. Moscow, 1924.

Poliakov, M.Ia., *Vissarion Grigor'evich Belinskii*. Moscow: Gosudarstvennoe uchebno-padagogicheskoe izdatel'stvo, 1960. Another high school text.

_____,*Poeziia kriticheskoe mysli. O masterstve Belinskogo i nekotorykh voprosakh literaturnoi teorii (The Poetry of the Critical Mind. On Belinskii's Profession and Several Questions of Literary Theory)*. Moscow: Sovetskii pisatel', 1968.

_____,*Vissarion Belinskii, lichnost', idei, epokha (Vissarion Belinskii, Personality, Ideas, Times)*. Moscow: Gosudarstvennoe izdatel'stvo khudozhestvennoi literatury, 1960.

Pypin, A.N., *Belinskii, ego zhizn i perepiska (Belinskii, His Life and Correspondence)*, 2nd Edition. St. Petersburg: knizhnoe izdatel'stvo "Kolos", 1908. The first scholarly work to publish the more subversive letters, newly possible in the relaxed censorship after the Revolution of 1905.

Raikhin, D.Ia., *Belinskii v shkole; posobie dlia uchitelei srednei shkolu (Belinskii in School: an Aid for Teachers of Middle Schools)*. Moscow, Gosudarstvennoe uchebno-pedagogicheskoe izdatel'stvo, 1966. Still another school text.

Sharypov, N.A., *Ateizm V.G. Belinskogo (The Atheism of V.G. Belinskii)*. Moscow: Vyshaia shkola, 1961. A high school text for courses on materialist ideology.

Smirnov. Z.V., *Obshchestvenno-politicheskie i folosofskie vzgliady V.G. Belinskogo (Social-Political and Philosophical Views of V.G. Belinskii)*. Moscow: Znamie, 1952. A widely used late Stalinist pamphlet which has been translated into English (see previous section).

Stepanishchev, S.S., *Razvitie obshchesvennoi mysli v trudakh russkikh revoliutionerov-demokratov (The Development of Social Thought in the Works of Russian Revolutionary Democrats)*. Minsk: Vyshaia shkola, 1975. Another high school text.

Stepanov, V.I., *Filosofskie i sotsiologicheskie vozzreniia V.G. Belinskogo (The Philosophical and Sociological Views of V.G. Belinskii)*. Minsk: Belorusskii gosudarstvennyi universitet, 1959.

Tal'nikov, D.L., *Teatral'naia estetika Belinskogo (Belinskii's Aesthetics of the Theatre)*. Moscow: Iskusstvo, 1962.

V.G. Belinskii v portretakh, illiustratsiiakh, dokumentakh (V.G. Belinskii in Portraits, Illustrations, Documents), edited by A.M. Gordin. Leningrad, Gosudarstvennoe uchebno-pedagogicheskoe izdatel'stvo, 1958.

Zdravomyslov, B.V., *Ugolovno-pravovye vzgliady russkikh revoliutsionykh demokratov (The Views of the Russian Revolutionaries on Criminal Justice)*. Moscow: Gosudarstvennoe izdatel'stvo iuridicheskoi literatury, 1959.

BELINSKII IN IMAGINATIVE LITERATURE

Gaetskii, Iu. A., *K dalekomy utru, povest' o Belinskom (Toward the Distant Dawn: a Story about Belinskii)*. Moscow: Gosudarstvennoe izdatel'stvo detskoi literatury, 1961. A story for children.

Serebrovskaia, E.P., *Ia i mire-boets, povest' o zhizni Vissariona Belinskogo (The World-Fighter and Me: a Story of the Life of Vissarion Belinskii)*. Moscow: Molodaia gvardiia, 1964. A story for young people.

Slavin, L.I., *Neukrotimyi. Povest' o V. Belinskogo (The Indomitable: a Story of V. Belinskii)*. Moscow: Politizdatel'stvo, 1973. A story for adults.

There is also said to have been a play, *Lermontov*, by V.V. Larvenёv, originally performed in 1953, containing several scenes between Lermontov and Belinskii.